D0422626

To my mom and dad,
I love you.

CONTENTS

THE PAGES AHEAD

You take some wood and wire, you make a box (sort of) in the shape of a figure eight, then you play it.

Sounds simple, but a guitar is a mystery of creative genius. Who was the first to imagine the music it could make? Who discovered that if you use Brazilian rosewood on the back and spruce on top, your instrument will resonate with richness? Who determined the exact width and tension you'd need for a wire to ring out a clear F-sharp?

I'm not sure who first created this wonderful stringed instrument, but I think the world's a better place for it. From classical concertos to rock and roll anthems, from a campfire on the beach to Carnegie Hall, the guitar might just be the most versatile and dearly loved instrument of our time.

Wait. No, I think there is another instrument that is definitely more important and dearly loved than the guitar. It's the instrument you see every morning when you look in the mirror—you. And although I don't know who created the guitar, I *do* know who created you. Almighty God, formed you with His hands. Psalm 139:13–14 testifies:

> For you created my inmost being;
>> you knit me together in my mother's womb.
> I praise you because I am fearfully and wonderfully made;
>> your works are wonderful,
>> I know that full well.

You're not some lucky combination of molecules that happened one day to crawl out of the muck onto dry land. Every cell and system in your being has care, purpose, and genius written all over it. Listen again to Psalm 139:

> How precious to me are your thoughts, O God!
>> How vast is the sum of them!
> Were I to count them,
>> they would outnumber the grains of sand. (vv. 17–18)

And you were made for more than this world sells. All that this world has to offer—no matter how appealing it is at the time—is temporary. It leaves us still hungry, wanting more, because we were made for something greater. We were created to shine the spotlight on God—to spread the fame of God everywhere we go.

I wrote this book to encourage you along your journey.

In the pages ahead, I'll tell some stories and share some truths and life lessons. And I'll introduce you to some of the people who've encouraged me the most along my road. People like:

- Louie Giglio, founder of the Passion Movement and sixstepsrecords, mentor and leader to thousands, songwriter, friend.
- Shelley, Louie's wife and partner in ministry, and our band's able (and very patient) manager. She knows everything about all the important things that were supposed to happen hours ago, and she's still calm. I don't get it.
- Jesse Reeves, bass player, songwriting partner, Traveller (the name of my band), friend. He said he'd play just one time with me—that was in Lufkin, Texas—and we've been playing together ever since.
- Daniel Carson, guitar player, kid wonder, Traveller. If you want to know how to tour full-time while you're still in high school, he's the guy to ask.

- My parents, Connie and Donna Tomlin, my brothers, Ryan and Cory, and a grandparent or two.
- Ed Cash, producer of our newest album, *Arriving*.
- J. D. Walt, friend, songwriter, pastor.
- Some friends at Austin Stone Community Church.

When you finish, I hope you'll decide, *"Wow, if God can use that Chris guy, then I am way ahead of the curve!"* And even more, my prayer is that you'll discover in these precious days that you have been created for a great life—a life that tells the story of God.

...YOU HAVE BEEN CREATED FOR A GREAT LIFE—
A LIFE THAT TELLS THE STORY OF GOD.

top: In concert with my band, The Travellers
above: A promo poster

CHAPTER ONE

THE SOUND YOU HEAR

That sound you hear—the music that's changing our generation—where did it come from? If you were asked to find its roots, reproduce its sound, what would you do? Where would you go?

I wonder.

You might reach for an upright piano or a Stratocaster.

You might tell me about a man in black rocking the house at Folsom Prison.

You might want to pull out some vinyl from those great old labels like Blue Note, or Motown, or Sun Records.

You might want to take me back to the mountains of eastern Kentucky. Or to the little white churches of New England. Or to the slave ships and cotton fields…

If I could, I'd take you all the way back to the music of King Jehoshaphat. It was 800 B.C. or so, huge enemy armies had lined up against King Jehoshaphat, and he knew he was in big trouble.

Maybe you know the story. King Jehoshaphat couldn't think of a thing to do except pray. But when he did, God gave him a plan. The plan was music—but not just any music. A particular *kind* of music. "Sure," God told King Jehoshaphat, "send your soldiers out to battle, but send your musicians first. And tell them to lead the army into battle with worship songs."

Interesting plan of attack, don't you think? Unlike your average Hollywood movie, the music in this story wasn't meant to be the soundtrack for the big fight. It *was* the fight. Worship was their entire battle plan.

"Just sing out," Jehoshaphat told his men. So they did. "Praise the LORD," they sang, walking off to battle, "for His mercy endures forever" (2 Chronicles 20:21, NKJV).

Killer music, I guess you could say, because the whole enemy army was wiped out without Israel ever lifting a sword.

If you asked me what music is changing our times, I'd say it's worship like that.

I'd point to another Bible story—this time, to a jail cell in Philippi, where two beat-up evangelists sang hymns through the night. You might know this story too. Not long into Paul and Silas's little worship service, the earth started shaking. Then the chains broke, and the doors to their freedom swung open.

What a breakout that was! Even the jailer in charge of the prison got saved, along with his whole family.

Call it music to shake your world. Music to set your generation free. Music—and a whole life to go with it—that you and I were uniquely created for. That's what I want to explore with you in this book.

Have you heard the sound I'm talking about—filling a church or arena, rolling in waves out across a field at a festival, or whispered around a campfire? Have you experienced the revolution I'm talking about firsthand? God is still using worship to turn people around, to stop the enemy in his tracks.

Or a city. Take New York, for example.

Taking It to the City

New York City is quite a place. You can hear almost every language in the world on the sidewalks there. And along with Boston, New York is at the heart of college life in America—I'm told there are 900,000+ college students within a seventy-five-mile radius of Times Square.

We had wanted to take a Passion Movement worship event into the heart of the city for a long time. Of course, it's one thing to take worship events to college towns in the South and Midwest. These days you know you'll probably get a crowd. But New York is different. It's a world away from the Bible Belt, for one thing, and it's a ton more expensive.

We prayed, planned, and waited. But the doors to New York remained shut.

Until one afternoon last April. My band and I walked out of the Newark airport and took a cab to uptown Manhattan. We were headed for the legendary Beacon Theatre, on Broadway and 74th, where the next day we were going to be part of putting on our first-ever worship event for New York City college kids.

Here's what had happened. College students across the country had stepped up to help open the door. You see, over the past months of the Passion Tour, we had been taking an offering at every concert to pay for a free event in Boston. Churches and students from Sacramento to Madison caught the vision and chipped in. Then, at the concert in Boston, we challenged the students there—who aren't known for being fond of New Yorkers—to help present a gift of a free worship concert to students in the Big Apple.

They responded generously, and here we were, driving up Broadway, anxious to see what God would do next.

Or course, we had no idea what that might be. The Beacon, on New York's Upper West Side, has been a premier music venue for decades. The week before our date, Sting had been the ticket. The previous night, it had been

Ruben Studdard of *American Idol*. The night following, it would be the Irish phenom Damien Rice. Our concert had been advertised on campuses around the city. But we didn't know how well-known the music of Passion was in New York. And when you don't have advance ticket sales, you don't know who—if anyone—is going to show up.

But show up they did.

"NEVER HAD THIS KIND OF SHOW BEFORE…"

At 8:00 the next morning, when we went back to the Beacon to set up, kids were already lining up. Curious drivers going by on Broadway were slowing down for a look, backing up traffic. By afternoon, the line wound around several blocks. And the doors didn't open until seven!

You have to wonder what other New Yorkers were thinking. An MTV special? A release party for some hot new L.A. band? No, just students who couldn't wait to proclaim to their city the splendor of the Lord.

That night the place was packed. Thousands of students—so happy to be there, so hungry for God, *so* ready. And as soon as Charlie Hall opened, it was clear the crowd knew the songs, and they wanted to sing.

Loud!

After Charlie was finished, Louie welcomed everyone, then we broke into small groups for a prayer time. Everybody praying at the same time, out loud, for their campuses, for their city. I tell you, that's a beautiful sound.

Then our band came on for a forty-five-minute set. What can I say? Wish you coulda been there! It was so powerful. I felt as if the crowd was saying, "Hey Chris, just start the songs. We'll take it from there!" It was a worship leader's dream. I think those students sang better—and with more heart—than any place I've ever been. In fact, Joey, our video guy, told me later, "That was the first time I couldn't hear you play, Chris. People were so loud!"

Louie's message that night was about shining a light in the world. But it is a light that isn't our own. "Be the moon," he challenged. "You don't have any light on your own. We only reflect the light of Another. But when you and I get in the right place, Christ shines in us."

When the David Crowder Band came on to play the closing set, a theater manager who had been standing backstage came up and wanted to talk. "I've never seen anything like this," he said. "I had to step outside and call my dad." Turns out his dad runs the theatre, and the guy had worked there for years. "I just had to tell my dad that in all our years we've never had this kind of show.

All the drug-filled concerts that come through here—they can't begin to light up the place like this!"

He leaned closer. There was something else he wanted to tell me. "Man, I just went out in the crowd and sang!" he said, grinning self-consciously. "'Course, I don't know any of the songs. But I just felt something in my heart."

Two days later, John Leland of the *New York Times* wrote a feature on the event. He called it "Christian Music's New Wave Caters to Audience of One." "The worship gathering for college students reflects a ground-swell both within churches and in the Christian music marketplace," he wrote. "The musicians—who call them-selves 'worship leaders' rather than performers—sing not about God, but to God. The audience sings as much as they do."

New Wave? Old Wave?

Ask Jehoshaphat, or Paul and Silas, or the angels gathered at God's throne from the beginning of time. I think it's the real music of our past and of our eternal future, and it's happening now.

STAND IN AWE

This book is about the sound of a generation waking up to the big idea of worship as a way of life. One place you find this lifestyle expressed in the Bible is in a prayer of the prophet Habakkuk:

> LORD, I have heard of your fame;
> I stand in awe of your deeds, O LORD.
> Renew them in our day. (3:2)

When we see God for who He really is, we stand in awe—and we know that nothing less will ever do. Here's another Bible passage that shows how we should respond to God's fame:

> Yes, LORD, walking in the way of your laws,
> we wait for you;
> your name and renown
> are the desire of our hearts. (Isaiah 26:8)

The Bible clearly shows us that you and I have been uniquely created for a purposeful life, but—here's the un-American part—*it's not meant to be about us or our career or our fame. It's all about God and His glory.*

Think of yourself, then, as one of God's fame builders. That's what Jehoshaphat did on the battlefield. And Paul and Silas in prison. You and I are formed from the dust of His creation and given breath for this reason: *to spread*

His renown to everyone we meet by what we say and do.

It's the way I was made. It's the way you were made too. But something has gotten us off track.

SOMEBODY GOT TRADED

Maybe we've traded in the Person who made us and the reason He made us for the *things* He made. It's a powerful human tendency. Paul described it this way:

> For although they knew God, they neither glorified him as God nor gave thanks to him.... They exchanged the truth of God for a lie, and worshiped and served created things rather than the Creator. (Romans 1:21, 25)

These verses have always hit me hard. I see this powerful human tendency in me too. The pull of my wants, my needs, my possessions, my money, my time, my friends, my "career"—almost everything is about *me*, the created being, and not my God, the Creator.

Worship isn't really a churchy word. Everyone worships something. And what you worship is whatever you place the highest value on. It's what you order your choices by. What you surrender your will to. So, while most of us say,

"Hey, you won't find any stone idols at my house!" we don't really own up to what we *do* worship. Is it really God, our Creator, the One who asks for *all* of us?

Sin does such a number on us. It deceives us. It puts hooks into our pride, our insecurities, our fears, our selfishness. We set off through life trying to make it on our own. And forty years later we look back and think, *What did all that add up to? Not much!*

Let's face it, even at church we can trade in the real thing for the imitation:

Our meeting together in the name of Jesus can turn into a program.

Our songs to Him can turn into a performance for each other.

Our fellowship can turn into hanging out with "the right people."

Even our Gospel can become an insurance policy, a handy plan to get God on your side so you can have the life *you* really want.

The message of this book—and of every song I hope to write—is that it's time for this generation to let go of the imitations. Let go of the second-rate stuff. Let go of stuff, period. And reach for the real life we've been created for.

God didn't make a mistake when He made you. He didn't set out to make another Einstein or Mother Teresa or Michael Jordan or Michael W. only to get interrupted, say, or have a bad day and—*Oops! Lookey here. It's Billy. How disappointing.*

It's not like that at all. He's not wishing—not for a moment—that you could just get it together enough to be someone else. And He's not plugging His ears to your prayers just because you have some major screwups on your record.

He made you just the way you are for an extraordinary purpose, an unusual life—one that only you can live for Him.

"I WANT TO BE THE WAY I WAS MADE"

For me, a lot of it has to do with words and music. Singing and writing songs and leading others in worship are at the core of my calling as a child of God. There's nothing about these gifts and interests that make me better or worse than the next guy. But I'd be having a sorry excuse for a life if I didn't take them seriously.

What about you? I invite you to think prayerfully about the way *you* have been made as you read this book.

Let me tell you how the song "The Way I Was Made" from my most recent album, *Arriving,* came to be.

I'd just met my new producer, Ed Cash. He's a regular

kind of guy with an amazing range of gifts. By regular, I mean he usually looks like he just came back from duck hunting. By amazing, I mean he has a hot reputation in Nashville for his producing genius. He thinks in melody. He plays every instrument he picks up and plays it like a master. He sings like he should be on tour.

And he's honest. I think the second sentence out of his mouth when I met him was, "I always think of worship songs as, oh, *subpar*."

Okay. So we got that cleared up.

But I plunged ahead anyway. Before long, there I am in his studio, pouring out my heart on my guitar, showing him the best I have to offer.

After seventeen or eighteen songs that I thought might work on the new album, Ed reluctantly asked if he could play something for me. I said sure.

From the first guitar chord, I was swept away. Here's the little chorus Ed sang:

I want to live like there's no tomorrow
I want to dance like no one's around
I want to sing like nobody's listening
Before I lay my body down
I want to give like I have plenty

I want to love like I'm not afraid
I want to be the man I was meant to be
I want to be the way I was made.

When he was done, he handed me a scrap of paper with the chords and lyrics written on it. "See what you can do with this," he said. He'd written the piece quite a while ago, he said, but he couldn't seem to take it any further. "You take it and write the rest of it."

That got me thinking. *I want to be the man I was meant to be / I want to be the way I was made...* I really loved the emotion in those words. They just settled down into my spirit like a pebble sinking in a pond.

That afternoon I took the chorus home with me and went to work with Jesse on the rest of the song. It didn't take us long before we had captured something special. Here are the verses that soon rang from Apt 9B:

Verse 1

Caught in the half light / I'm caught alone
Waking up to the sunrise / and the radio
Feels like I'm tied up / what's holding me
Praying today will be the day I go free

Verse 2

Made in Your likeness, made with Your hands
Made to discover, who You are and who I am
All I've forgotten, help me to find
All that You've promised let it be in my life

I wonder if you recognize that feeling of knowing—knowing with all your heart and soul—that you desperately need to wake up to who God is and who He means for you to be.

LOOKING DOWN THE ROAD

That strong desire is at the heart of this book. Sure, life is hard. No one gets through without facing huge risks, without failing at times, without getting hurt. But even so, God made us to live a *full* life. Jesus said, "I have come that they may have life, and have it to the full" (John 10:10).

In the pages ahead I want to help you discover more about what God has uniquely made you to do and enjoy. Like a lot of young people, you might be looking ahead, down the road of your life, and wondering, *Does God really have something good in mind for my future—and if He does, do I want it?* Or, *Is a life lived for God's glory really as good as it gets?*

In the process of looking at those questions with you, I'll share a lot of personal stories. I'm not a preacher. And anyway, I've noticed that I often learn the most from other people's stories. But every word here is intended to encourage the young men and women of my generation to reach for the full and passionate life that God is calling us to.

It's a big road ahead.

But we have a big God.

top left: My dad taught me to love music early.
top right: Louie Giglio, mentor and Bible teacher

CHAPTER TWO

SALT OF THE EARTH

I f you had rolled into Grand Saline, Texas, in the early eighties, you might have heard the roar of Honda three-wheelers at full throttle. That would be my friends and me flying across the salt flats near our hometown.

The boys are grown now, and the three-wheelers are banned. But the salt remains.

Grand Saline means "Big Salt." But the town is small—an out-of-the-way East Texas town that happens to be the Texas home of the Morton Salt Company. You know the little girl with a yellow dress, holding an umbrella attached to the slogan "When it rains, it pours"? Yep, that's my town.

We even have a block of salt on the corner of Main Street and the highway. That's right, *the* highway. There's only one running through the middle of town. Seems like some family was always stopped at that block of salt. All the kids just had to touch it—or lick it (gross).

Grand Saline is one of those towns, you know, where Santa Claus rides the fire truck in *every* parade, not just the Christmas parade. And we had quite a few. We had the Salt Festival, the Salt Rodeo, and the Salt Parade. Of course every young woman growing up in Grand Saline dreamed of wearing that most coveted of crowns, that of the Salt Queen.

So I grew up knowing a little about small towns and salt. But, like most kids growing up, I didn't know that God was near. Only looking back now can I see that He was close to me during those years—close enough to speak through my parents, close enough to know my heart's desire and give it to me…

Right after He—or maybe it was another kid at school—gave me mononucleosis.

GUITAR DREAMS

I was nine years old the summer I got sick. Before long, staying indoors was driving me and everyone in the house crazy. One day Dad said, "Son, do you want to learn to play the guitar or the fiddle? I'm going to step outside for a minute, and when I come back in, I'd like to know." Dad was a practical man (a pharmacist, to be exact).

Truthfully, though, he never got to the porch. "Guitar!" I blurted out. It was that quick.

The same day, Dad brought home a classical guitar from his drugstore. To me it looked just like Willie Nelson's, minus the worn-through hole in the sound board.

That night Dad gave me my first lesson. Every night thereafter he wrote out guitar chords and notes for me to learn. Every morning after he went to work, I would start to practice, and I'd stay at it all day. When he came home, he would listen to me play. Then he'd give me more to practice.

Since Dad had an impressive collection of Willie on vinyl LPs, my repertoire filled up pretty quickly with Willie tunes. Two of my first songs were "Blue Eyes Crying in the Rain" and "On the Road Again." From there I branched out to other classics—Merle Haggard and Alabama, for example.

I know, I know. But God works in mysterious ways, doesn't He? It was no accident that I had gotten sick. God was working out His plan.

Meanwhile, Dad tried to help me keep the big picture in mind. "Remember, son," he'd say, "this is just a hobby." Like I said, he was a practical man. He had high hopes that my life would actually add up to something.

Problem was, my hobby was becoming more and more of an obsession. By the time I was fourteen, I had entered the garage band era. My band was a Stryper rip-off. We called ourselves the Seventh Seal, which is Revelation code talk for "the wrath of God." It seemed to fit our sound.

I'll tell you, right away we *did* have a sound. If I had to describe it, I would say "unbearable to human ears." Our introductions usually went something like, "Hi, we're the Seventh Seal, wrath of God…" And then I'd hit a power chord on my red, heavy-metal Ibanez guitar.

Our lead singer was a girl named Lisa. There wasn't any guy around who could hit the high notes our "sound" required, so she got the job.

J. J., our drummer, was full-on rock and roll. This was the era of "bring every drum you have and set it up for the concert," so J. J. always took up most of the stage.

Jason played the keyboards because he was the only one of us that had one. He basically played two sounds— helicopter and wind. Most every song started with the helicopter taking off. Then somewhere at the right moment, you'd hear the wind start to howl.

We were ahead of our time.

Seventh Seal's big debut was the midweek lunch slot of the Salt Festival. I was so nervous I could barely think. And I'll never forget the sound that came out of my guitar on our first song—the most awful squawk I'd ever heard. I quickly looked down at my hands. They were on the right chord. And I knew I had just tuned it—what professional wouldn't tune up his guitar before walking onstage?

Well, being the pro that I was, I just smiled and played

on. Friends pointed. A few people screamed. But I thought for sure they were just getting into it, so I turned up the volume.

At the end of the song, when I could finally hear what my friends were trying to tell me, I discovered that I'd accidentally left a pick in the strings, thus the awful squawk.

Seventh Seal didn't last long.

My first try at actual stardom was with my brothers, both younger than me. Ryan was a natural on the drums, and Cory was learning the fiddle. Our big numbers consisted of "Great Balls of Fire" and "Wipe Out." We dubbed ourselves the Swinging Tomlin Brothers and thought we might be ready for the big time. So we put in for every talent show Mom or Dad heard about. When one finally let us in, we showed up in matching T-shirts and parachute pants.

Fame hit hard. And fast. After about the third outing, we pulled the plug.

That's okay. God was still at work. He knew that a musician needs more than an instrument and a power cord. As strange as it might sound, He knew that I needed to put all that down, along with all my dreams, and ask Him for something more important first.

And what was that? Of course, I didn't have a clue. But the Holy Spirit showed me. And not surprisingly, He used worship songs to do it.

Under a Tree, Shaking

I was at a church camp that summer. I always looked forward to camp, I think because in my heart I wanted more of God. And this was not your normal camp—we had plenty of fun, but the emphasis was on discipleship.

During one of the meetings, we spent some time singing worship songs. I remember that God seemed to be very near. He seemed to be using the songs to whisper into my deepest being. Then He seemed to open my heart and soul and show me—what? I didn't know. I didn't have any words for it.

So I bolted. I ran out of the service into the muggy Texas night. Honestly, I don't know if I was running away from God or running toward Him. But I knew He was pursuing me.

I ended up by myself under a tree, shaking (I could take you to that same tree today). I didn't know what to say. What *does* a boy going through puberty know to say to the Maker of Mountains, the Tamer of Oceans?

Finally, with tears and a willing heart, I began to cry out one of the most honest prayers I've ever prayed. It went something like this:

Lord, I don't know what to say to You, but I know You're speaking to me. You can have all of me. For the rest of my days, I want to live for You. Whatever You want, whatever You ask—it's Yours. I belong to You now. Amen.

I didn't ask God to make me happy or good or famous. I didn't ask Him to make me a musician or to put me onstage. And I'm so glad now that I didn't. I just handed over my life. I wanted to be His man.

Looking back, I see that moment as maybe the most important event in my preparation to serve God with music. Sooner or later, everyone has to settle "the ownership issue" (maybe you know what I mean). Whose life are you going to live—yours or God's? Whose name and honor will you invest your time and energy and passion in—yours or God's?

Paul wrote a lot about the ownership issue. For example:

I have been crucified with Christ and I no longer live, but Christ lives in me. (Galatians 2:20)

And,

[Christ] died for all, that those who live should no longer live for themselves but for him who died for them and was raised again. (2 Corinthians 5:15)

Wow, I love those verses! There's just no middle ground. What Paul is saying adds up to a radical exchange: "I was living for myself. Then I died to myself. Now I live for Christ. And it's even better than that—*Christ lives in me!*"

I'm not saying that once surrendered, you're always automatically surrendered. On a regular basis, and in many different areas, I still need to hand over to God my right to run my life. But I think an event of personal dedication is important. Mine matters to me. Something necessary and priceless happened that night. When my circumstances or feelings get confusing, I can point to it and feel genuinely grateful.

I hope you can point to a similar moment in your life. If you can't, ask God to lead you to it. Tell Him you're *that* serious about experiencing the life He created you for, which is *His life in you*. He'll answer, I know, because He wants that life for you even more than you do.

When you settle the ownership issue, you'll start to see mountains move.

I sure did.

TRAVELING MUSIC MAN

One afternoon when I was a senior in high school, a family friend and traveling music man, David Crain, dropped by my house. He was on his way to play in a concert in Texarkana and asked if I would like to come along and help sell tapes (notice I said "tapes"). I would be his roadie, so to speak.

I was pretty excited. Maybe this would be my big break in the music biz. Sure enough, the first night, in the middle of the concert, David stopped and asked me to come onstage and sing a song of my own.

I was terrified. If this was my big break, I wasn't in the least ready for it. We had driven three hours to get there, and David had never once mentioned anything to me about singing.

Reluctantly, I stood behind his keyboard and banged out one of the more awful live performances in the history of Texarkana.

But God was near. For some reason, a youth pastor who was there asked me to come and sing at his church. I couldn't believe it. Of course, I agreed. But all the time I was thinking to myself, *Man, the music in his church must really stink!*

That invitation turned into more invitations. Shortly afterward, I was invited to play at a weeklong crusade in East Texas. A week? I didn't have anywhere near enough material to last a week! I knew maybe five or six songs. Two of them were "Lean on Me" and "Pharaoh, Pharaoh."

But my life belonged to Someone Else, and I was just crazy enough to accept.

CRUSADING WITH JAMES LANKFORD

Then I got a phone call from a deep-voiced gentleman named James Lankford. He told me he would be the speaker at the crusade. He was calling to find out who I was and what kind of music I was planning for the event. He said he'd never heard of me.

I quickly answered that the reason he'd never heard of me was that I had never really done this before. But I assured him I had a few silver bullets in my musical arsenal. I mentioned "Lean on Me" and "Pharaoh, Pharaoh."

There was a long pause on the other end of the line.

"I'm going to send you a tape of some worship songs," he said finally. "You listen and tell me what you think. Then by crusade time, maybe you can be ready."

As soon as the tape (again, I say "tape") arrived, I dove in. The tape was called "Isn't He," produced by a guy named Louie Giglio. It was full of songs like "I Love You, Lord" and "More Precious than Silver"—worship standards for most people, but brand-new to me. I wrote out every song on its own note card, then added the guitar chords above each line. I figured I was ready for the crusade.

Each night of the crusade, I took the note cards and arranged them across the stage in the order I wanted to do the songs. Then, to make sure my "order of worship" wouldn't get blown away, I taped each one of them to the floor. The plan worked.

Sorta.

Each night, I would move the microphone stand down-line one song at a time, from left to right, as I sang through my play list. The beautiful thing was, no one knew my plan. Unless they wondered why I never looked at the crowd. Or always sang to my feet. Or, night after night, kept sliding to the right.

It's hilarious to think about now!

But James was patient. He was there to give me wisdom on what I did well and what I didn't do so well. The end of the week came, and we were sitting in his car talking. I remember that conversation well, because it was to be another moment in my life when God leaned very near.

"You're gifted, Chris," James said. "Of course, you have a lot to learn when it comes to leading people in worship." He paused. "But God has bigger plans for you than you can imagine now."

He reached over and put his hand on my head (that was weird). Then he prayed a simple, one-sentence prayer: "God, make Chris a psalm writer for his generation."

Those were more than just words to me. They washed over my heart. They went deep into my bones.

Time to Drop the Backup Plan

My college years took me first to a community college near home, then to Texas A&M. I had started to travel a bit with a guitar, a cheesy drum machine, and background tapes. The calls just kept coming in—how people heard about me is still a mystery. I didn't have any flyers or a website, much less any tapes. But there I was in my apartment, fielding invitations to come and play.

Those years presented a whole new set of challenges to my faith. In my case, I don't mean doubts that God existed but doubts that His plan for Chris Tomlin existed. And if it did, that I could find it. And if I did find it, that I could ever make a living doing it.

I had grown up in a very normal American family. You graduate from high school, go to college, major in a sensible—hopefully lucrative—career area; then once you graduate, you get a job, get married, and settle down to make money and kids.

Where exactly was the career path for a guy who wants to play a guitar, write some songs, drive wherever, and accept whatever people give him? I kept hearing my dad saying, "Now son, remember, this is just a hobby…"

And when it came to ever winning a bride, I kept imagining a scenario that went like this:

[Scene opens]

I am in a lineup of suitors for the girl of my dreams. I'm fidgety and dry-mouthed. My turn comes. I step in to meet the stern-faced father.

"And what do you do?" asks he from the other side of a huge desk.

"Ah, I travel around and play my guitar," responds me.

"Mmmmm. And what else do you do?" asks father. "What do you do for a living?"

"Ah, th-that *is* what I do…for a living…" My voice trails off.

Silence.

Then the father decides.

"NEXT!" he yells.

[End of scene]

I wonder if you've wrestled like that with your future. Most young people I know do. We see and believe—most of the time—that God made us for a reason and that He is at work in some general kind of way leading us toward it. But we just don't see the individual steps that could take us from here to there. So while our heart might be saying yes, our mind keeps burying us in doubts.

Looking back, I can see that God *was* hard at work on my real future. But at the time, I wasn't convinced. So I played it safe. I let God do His thing, and I went to work getting into physical therapy school. Not that I had a passion for it, but physical therapy seemed like a logical way for me to make money (just being honest).

One night I was on the phone catching up with Brad, a friend who'd moved away. He asked me how the music was going.

I told him it was going great, but I'd be hanging it up when I graduated, since if I made it into physical therapy school, my studies would be full-time and I'd have no more time to travel. But, I told Brad, I'd had fun while it lasted.

At that point, God Himself must have picked up the receiver and took over the conversation. I say this because Brad does not remember saying what I heard next: *Well, I guess we always have our own plan in case God's plan doesn't work out.*

Whatever Brad did say next, I didn't hear it. I saw with absolute clarity that I was stuck in a crisis of faith—and that if I didn't start taking steps in the right direction *whether or not I could guarantee the outcome*, I would never get where God wanted me to go.

It was time to drop the backup plan and go with what God was asking me to do.

COFFEE AT THE KETTLE

Of course, I still had a thousand questions and a thousand things to learn. But God kept opening doors and introducing me to the right people. People like Louie Giglio.

Remember Louie? He was the producer of that first little worship tape I had received in the mail a few years back. Little did I know at the time that God would bring us together. But while I'd been busy leading worship for a Bible study at Texas A&M called Breakaway, Louie was busy not far away leading a Bible study at Baylor University called Choice. God had been using Louie for some time to speak into the lives of university students about worship and devotion to the glory of God. Every Monday night, a lot of A&M students would drive over to Baylor for Louie's study. I did too. When I met Louie and then his wife, Shelley—now my manager—we hit it off right away.

The summer I graduated, Louie and I spent two weeks ministering together at a camp in Brownwood, Texas. Each night when we were done, we'd drop by the Kettle, a wannabe Waffle House, and the only restaurant around still open. We'd take a table, relax, and talk till all hours.

From the first night, I pumped Louie with questions. What was God doing in this generation? What might He want from me? And—getting strictly practical—if I kept on playing music and leading worship, how would I ever pay my bills?

I'll never forget his response to one of my questions.

"Louie," I asked, "how do you go about your scheduling? Do you have an agent? Do I need an agent?" Right there you can tell how much I didn't know.

"Yes," Louie answered, "I have an agent. His name is the Holy Spirit. He knows where I need to go, when I need to go there, and how much money I'll need to get there and back. You need the same agent."

Wow, I thought, *I like this guy*.

It was at the Kettle, and over the months following, that Louie shared his vision for a movement he called Passion. The passion Louie was talking about is described in what has become the movement's key text, Isaiah 26:8:

> Yes, LORD, walking in the way of your laws,
>   we wait for you;
> your name and renown
>   are the desire of our hearts.

Louie wasn't thinking small. He had a heart to see millions of college students across the nation awaken to the reality of a glorious God. "I'd really like you to be involved," he told me. I thought being a part of something that big would be amazing.

CELEBRATE HIS GREATNESS

And it has. In 1997, the first Passion event rolled out in Austin, Texas. Two thousand students showed up. It was a time of praise and adoration, prayer, confession, teaching, and celebration. The atmosphere was electric. After the main sessions, we broke out into smaller groups of three or four hundred people, one of which I led. Everyone left town knowing that God was up to something and that we all wanted to be part of it.

More Passion milestones followed. The next year, five thousand students came to Austin. From that event came the first CD, *Passion: Live Worship from the 268 Generation.* The next year it was 11,500 students in Fort Worth and another album, *Passion: Better Is One Day.* That led to the first OneDay gathering in May 2000 in Memphis—tens of thousands of college students representing every U.S. state and twenty-six foreign countries.

You have to ask, *What is God doing in this generation? What is rising among us? What unstoppable need of the Spirit is crying out?*

Ultimately, only God knows what He's accomplishing in our time. I just know I want to be a part of it, and I urge you to be too. I believe that as we lift up our sovereign God together to His rightful place in our lives and celebrate His greatness in our worship, all the lesser things fall away. And we stand before Him in wonder, ready—maybe for the first time—to live out our true created purpose for His glory.

"I KNOW THE PLANS I HAVE FOR YOU..."

As you can see, my testimony is basically that God has faithfully placed people in my path who saw something in me and believed in me—believed in me enough to invest their lives. It's been almost a decade now since I met Louie and Shelley. They have graced me with the best friendship, creative teamwork, and ministry partnership I could imagine. In that time, God has allowed me to realize the dream to record albums. And He has graciously blessed songs I've written and recorded for the personal and corporate worship of millions of His people—songs like "Forever" and "We Fall Down" and "Famous One."

Let me be the first to say that it's not about me—it's all about Him! Praise His name! He is the faithful One.

Could the nine-year-old boy growing up in Grand Saline, Texas, picking away on his drugstore guitar, even hope that such a time would come? Could a teenager giving all his dreams away to God one night under a tree expect to get any of them back? Could a traveling evangelist—who had to put up with some pretty lame music outings with me—ever know that God would work mightily through his spoken words of blessing?

In the pages ahead, I want to share more of my personal story. Honestly, I really only have one purpose—and it's not to dwell on any successes or failures that may have come my way. I want to speak a blessing into your life in the same way my parents and James Lankford and Louie and others have done for me. Because there's something you need to remember through every question, confusion, or uncertainty in the days ahead:

Right now, the God who made you knows your heart, knows your desires, your strengths, your limitations...and this God has only good in mind for your future. Through Jeremiah God told His people, "'I know the plans I have for you,' declares the LORD, 'plans to prosper you and not to harm you, plans to give you hope and a future'" (Jeremiah 29:11).

Of course, it only makes sense that you would want to know this God well enough to trust His intentions for you. So in the next chapter I want to take you on what you might call a "songwriting road trip" about God's nature.

I know. Sounds a little unusual.

But musicians get to be that way.

above: I guess I always had a goal in mind.
right: My Grandpa Duncan blesses me with his prayers.

CHAPTER THREE

MADE FOR HIS GLORY

We sing a lot today about wanting to see God. This is a good thing to sing. We want to experience Him more fully. We want a face, a touch, a word…

But do we have any idea what seeing and hearing God firsthand would actually be like?

I think I got a little glimpse at our Passion OneDay student gathering, Memorial Day 2003.

It was Saturday evening just outside of Sherman, Texas. Thousands of students were busy setting up their tents in a field. I was there in a tent too, huddled for a planning session with about forty of the leadership team. I guess we were all distracted, not really paying attention to what was rolling down on us.

When the Texas-sized thunderstorm hit the field, lightning cracked and thunderclaps shook the ground. Then the rain hit and campers dove for cover. A deafening roar of wind, water, lightning, and thunder swept over all of us. The only thing we could do was to hold on and wait.

Well, the roar put a stop to our meeting. We were inches apart, but we couldn't hear each other speak. So for about an hour we prayed—hands raised, lips moving silently in the roar. We were praying for God to rescue our plans, to stop the storm. At least, that's what I was praying. Surely this thunderstorm wasn't God's idea. Would He want to shake up all these campers? And maybe scare a few back to California? It was a wild night.

But when Beth Moore opened up the gathering on Memorial Day, she had a different perspective on the storm. She said that everyone involved with OneDay had prayed and prayed for God to "send His glory," that we earnestly wanted to meet with Him in these days, on this very field! So, she asked, did you notice God's answer? That storm was God telling us, "I am arriving!"

Those three words that stopped me in my "I-have-God-figured-out" tracks. Beth was right. In all that flash and roar, God was coming near, near enough to let us get a physical experience of what we usually only know in our spirits—that He is truly *awesome*!

Did you know that the word *awesome* can be translated in the Hebrew as *terrifying*?

When Isaiah saw God seated on His throne, he cried out, "Woe to me! I am ruined!" (Isaiah 6:5). Revelation 4:5

states, "From the throne came flashes of lightning, rumblings and peals of thunder." To come that close to God would be a truly *awesome* experience.

I will never again think of that word the same. I will never sing that word the same. It is truly a word we should reserve for God only.

TRAITS AND TUNES

You and I can never remain the same after we see who God really is. And that's why I want to talk about God's nature in this chapter. Who is this God who made us and who calls us to give ourselves to Him? What is He like?

I'm not asking stuffy theological questions here. These questions lie at the heart of my music. They're what I sing about every day. So in this chapter I want to try to do two things at once:

- Talk about a few of God's character traits that I think about most and;
- Talk about them by sharing some of my songs and the stories behind them.

Does this approach sound weird? Okay, but think about it. It's *the way I'm made*—to know who God is and to bring to Him in worship all that He's made me to be (in my case—guitar player, singer, small-town boy, risk taker, to pick a few). That's the Chris Tomlin-life that most pleases God and most fulfills me as I live it by His grace.

I'm often asked how I write my songs. It's hard to put into exact language. I like how a songwriter named Dennis Jernigan explains it: He says he isn't so much a songwriter as a song *receiver*. I think that's closer to it for me, because at its core, writing a worship song is a lot like receiving a gift, or responding to an awakening in me toward God.

But there's a flip side to that. Like most things in life, you don't just wake up one day and decide you're now a world-renowned songwriter. You don't pick up a guitar one morning and expect to be Chet Atkins by lunch. It takes practice. There's holy work involved. For me, *a lot* of holy work and unholy sweat (and I'll still never touch Chet).

Generally, I think writing good worship songs takes some knowledge of how chord structures and melodies work together. Then you need to sense how to move them forward in a sequence or progression that will shape a satisfying song. But most of all it takes an open and sensitive heart to the Spirit of God.

Another common question is, "Which comes first, the melody or the lyric?" For me, bizarre as it sounds, they usually come together. And as to how *that* happens—sorry, I just don't know.

My songs usually start from the audience's perspective. I mean, I don't consider them my artistic masterpieces that no one better mess with. They're not mine at all. They're God's. They are meant to serve Him. So when I sit down to write something, I'm usually asking a couple of simple questions: "What do worshipers want to say or sing to God?" and, "What does God want to hear from them?"

Now maybe you can see why, for me at least, talking about who God is and how I wrote my songs about Him can go together.

Let's give it a try.

1. God is supreme.

Our increasingly me-centered culture has even influenced a lot of our worship songs. There's so much "me," "mine," "I," and "Lord, do this for me."

I'm not saying it's wrong or theologically incorrect to word a song like this. (If that were so, we would have to throw many of the Psalms out as well. David cries out to God about himself all through his songs.) It's just that we must be careful not to keep all the attention on us. But our flesh, our sinful selves, can confuse us. Confuse us into thinking that the world revolves around us, that somehow our desires should be at the center of our response to God.

In the Passion Movement, our calling is simply to align coming generations with Isaiah 26:8, which can be stated like this: "Yes, Lord, walking in Your truth, we wait eagerly for You, for Your name and renown are the desire of our souls."

That confession has "God-centered" all over it. Just the first two words put us in the right frame of mind—"Yes, Lord…"

I believe if we can just get a hold of the biggest possible picture of God, all the other things we care about in our lives will line up correctly. This might not sound like a great sell in today's me-centered world. But what's more relevant to you and me than God? Has the Creator who said "Let there be"—and there was—now lost His voice? Has the God who became flesh and blood in the person of Jesus and befriended everyday people like drunks and prostitutes and you and me now lost His touch?

No! God is still the most relevant being in the universe, and knowing Him is still the most important quest of our lives. Our worship should naturally reflect this. To put ourselves in first place is to fall way short and be continually disappointed.

The song "We Fall Down" was born when I became captivated by the picture the throne of God in Revelation 4. Here is this remarkable scene of elders falling down before the throne and laying their crowns at the feet of the Lamb. At the same time, you have something John calls "living creatures" (poor John, he was having a hard time describing these guys) proclaiming back and forth, day and night, "Holy, holy, holy is the Lord God Almighty, who was, and is, and is to come" (v. 8).

What a stunning picture of the glory and greatness of God!

After letting this vision of heaven sink in for a while, I grabbed my guitar and began to sing out these words:

We fall down
We lay our crowns
At the feet of Jesus

The greatness of
Mercy and love
At the feet of Jesus
And we cry holy, holy, holy
We cry holy, holy, holy
We cry holy, holy, holy
Is the Lamb

I wish I could tell you where the melody was coming from. I wish I could give you a five-step plan to finding a good melody. But I can't. That song was simply coming out of a worshiping heart.

Actually, I believe melodies and lyrics appear most readily in free souls. For instance, think of whistling. I actually can't whistle a thing, but I love to listen to my Grandpa Duncan do it. When he whistles, he isn't striving for a melody. He's just letting a tune come out naturally. That's why the best melodies come from a joyful, free heart.

2. God is holy.

It was early May 2003 (yes, a few weeks before that thunderstorm). I was preparing for the OneDay gathering coming up in Sherman. For some reason, a song from Isaiah 6 began to find its way into my ears and heart. You might be familiar with the text. It's what the seraphim were calling out to one another as they flew around the throne of God:

> Holy, holy, holy is the LORD Almighty;
> The whole earth is full of his glory. (Isaiah 6:3)

"At the sound of their voices," Isaiah wrote, "the doorposts and thresholds shook and the temple was filled with smoke" (Isaiah 6:4). What a concert that must have been!

Those words of worship rolled around inside me for about a week. Louie and I were in L.A. doing a TV show with a friend. I told him I had this chorus idea, but nothing more. He pointed me to Nehemiah 8, where I read about a throng of worshipers who stood in silence, hands raised to God, when their leaders read from the Word. Then the worshipers bowed with their faces to the ground.

What a picture! So unlike any I've seen before in our churches today. Louie went off to his room for the night, but I stayed up with my guitar. The scene had really hit home, and I began scribbling down thoughts as quickly as I could. When it came, "Holy Is the Lord" came easily. I think the angels were singing the melody to me. Within about fifteen minutes, it was finished.

We stand and lift up our hands
For the joy of the Lord is our strength
We bow down and worship Him now
How great, how awesome is He

It's rising up all around
It's the anthem of the Lord's renown

I still wasn't sure if the song was meant for OneDay, but just in case, I taught it to the band. When we got to Sherman, we were ready. I think. (I don't recommend trying out a new song for the first time in front of over twenty thousand people.)

Our band was supposed to follow John Piper, but I

hadn't gotten a chance to talk much with him beforehand. Next thing you know, he's on and we're backstage. I remember praying on my knees in the grass behind the stage, wondering which songs we should sing. Then I heard John say something astounding: "Students, God has put a message on my heart for you today, and it is Isaiah 6: 'Holy, holy, holy is the LORD Almighty, the whole earth is full of his glory.'"

Yes sir, John, I was thinking the same thing! But God knows I'm a little slow, so He made it obvious.

"Holy Is the Lord" was meant for that day, and for all other days too, because the truth of God's absolute holiness and earth-filling glory is timeless.

You might be thinking, *But God's holiness doesn't really lead me to worship. Actually, it leads me to keep my distance. It intimidates me because I'm so unholy.*

I sure understand this reaction. But let me pass on some encouragement. First—good news—you are not making up your problem. You are squarely in reality (at least on this issue) because you can't bridge the gap from your fallenness to God's holiness. Only Christ can do that for us. Therefore, when we really see the holiness of God— the complete otherness of Him—it's right that we tremble.

But consider this: This holy, holy One, from whose throne come flashes of lightning and peals of thunder—*this very God* draws you and me to Himself. Just to be allowed, much less invited, into His presence is proof of His incredible mercy and love.

And it gets even better: This same holy God sees all His children dressed only in the spotless white of Christ's holiness.

Think about that for a while. Think about it all night. Drink it in all day. Build your life on it. And I promise that the wonder of God's holiness will get you on your feet, or on your face, in His presence.

3. God is forever.

Have you ever had one of those brain-freeze moments when thinking about eternity? I mean, just how long *is* forever? How can mortals like you and me really grasp that we are living beings with a spirit and soul inside of us that is eternal? It's beyond our feeble minds. At least beyond mine.

Of course, when I was sixteen I thought I'd live forever, but as the years have rolled by, I understand Psalm 103:15–16 better: "As for man, his days are like grass, he flourishes like a flower of the field; the wind blows over it and it is gone, and its place remembers it no more."

Still, I want my "days like grass" to count for something. God didn't make us to just live out some boring routine all our days. No, we were made in His image, and we are eternal because God is eternal. His character and integrity will never waver. We can trust our days—and our eternity—to His nature.

That's why I love singing and playing "Forever" night after night. Each time we strike the first A chord, I'm reminded of my destiny. The song grew out of Psalm 136: "Give thanks to the LORD, for he is good. His love endures *forever*" (v. 1).

And true to the title, the song took me about forever to write. I had the verses and the "sing praise" channel from the start, but never had a good chorus. Nothing really finished the thought. Oh, I had many choruses, but they were all horrible. Maybe I was trying to be too artsy or something. Whenever I took the song to the studio, the producers would say things like, "It's *going* to be a great song." A guy can start to hate that kind of encouragement.

Finally one summer, when our band was playing at a camp, I revisited the song. I kept thinking to myself, *Just keep it simple. Come back to the heart of the song.*

The chorus finally landed like this...

Forever God is faithful
Forever God is...
Forever God is with us
Forever

I began to get a little excited. The chorus actually seemed to be taking shape. But that second line stopped me. It should have been so simple, but nothing would come.

Forever God is faithful
Forever God is…what?

I'd start over.

Forever God is faithful
Forever God is…

Believe it or not, I struggled with that line for days looking for the right word.

Forever God is…

One night I was sitting on my bed, guitar in hand, struggling away, when the door to my room burst open. There stood Janet Reeves, Jesse's wife. She and Jesse had been in the next room. My constant repetitions of the unfinished lyric had finally driven her over the edge. She said politely, "Chris, the word you're looking for is *strong*."

I fell on the floor laughing. She had been listening to my wrestling match with the English language, patiently waiting for me to find the obvious, right word—and finally realized I wasn't going to find it without help.

"Forever" has been such a surprise song. It was one of those that, while it's coming, you feel people will want to sing it. But I had no idea the impact this song would have. It's being sung all over the world, in many languages. That kind of service to God's people is worth a very long wait.

4. God is…enough.

We were getting ready for the Passion Tour in 2001—our first road trip ever. It actually started on September 11, 2001, of all days. The whole nation was reeling in horror and grief…and God had us out on the highway taking the message of His goodness to the masses. Isn't that just like Him? To put a bunch of people who have never toured before on the road in the middle of one of our nation's hardest times?

Just before the start of the tour, I asked Louie in passing if he had had any lyric ideas lately. He usually has scribblings lying around. He did this time. Something he'd written in his journal came to mind. He said he had been praying the words to God lately. He tore the page out of his journal and handed it to me. "See if anything hits you," he said. "Maybe it could be something for the tour."

Of course, I had to spend a little time translating Louie's handwriting. But this is what I made out:

All of you
Is more than enough
For all of me
For every thirst
For every need

Then he had a list of different attributes of God written underneath. Interrupting these attributes was this line, which particularly caught my attention:

And still more awesome than I know

What a huge thought! No matter how much I know and see about God, He is still greater than I can comprehend!

Later that night, when I began to work on the song, the melody for "Enough" just seemed to fall out on the page.

The thought that God is more than enough for us is an understatement in itself. The English language can only go so far in describing someone this indescribable. But I've heard of someone who got as close as you can get. It's part of a sermon by the late Dr. S. M. Lockridge, an

African-American who was a pastor in San Diego for forty years. It is powerful! You'll love it!

Well, David says, "The heavens declare the glory of God and the firmament showeth His handiwork." My King is a sovereign king. No means of measure can define His limitless love. No far-seeing telescope can bring into visibility the coastline of His shoreless supply. No barrier can hinder Him from pouring out His blessings. He's enduringly strong. He's entirely sincere. He's eternally steadfast. He's immortally graceful. He's imperiously powerful. He's impartially merciful.

And I wonder…do you know Him?

He's the greatest phenomenon that has ever crossed the horizon of this world. He's God's Son. He's the sinner's Savior. He's the centerpiece of civilization. He stands in the solitude of Himself. He's matchless, He's unique. He's unparalleled, He's unprecedented. He's the loftiest idea in literature. He's the highest personality in philosophy. He's the supreme problem in higher criticism. He's the fundamental doctrine in true theology. He's the cardinal necessity of the spiritual religion. He's the miracle of the ages. He's the superlative of every good thing that you choose to call Him; and He's the only one qualified to be an all-sufficient Savior...

Well, my King's the key to knowledge. He's the wellspring of wisdom. He's the doorway to deliverance. He's the pathway to peace. He's the roadway to righteousness. He's the highway to holiness. He's the gateway to glory. That's my King.

I wish I could describe Him to you, but He's indescribable! That's what He is, He's indescribable! He's incomprehensible! He's invincible! He's irresistible!

You can't get Him out of your head. You can't get Him off your hands. You can't outlive Him, and you can't live without Him...

That's my King and I wonder...do you know Him?

LIVING IN WONDER OF HIM

Do you stand in awe this moment at the greatness, the wonder, the goodness of our King? I hope so. A life that's grounded in that amazing reality just can't look the same as one that's built on puny self-centered concerns. That's what I want to look at in the next chapter.

Now that we've had a glimpse of Him, what would your life and mine look like if we set out each day to truly live in wonder of Him?

above: Going for the big ones with Billy Foote.

CHAPTER FOUR

LIFESTYLES OF THE UNNOTICED

I t's time for Christians to get serious about fame. Really. Fame matters (come on, admit it). You can feel it, measure it, maybe even get rich off it. Some people turn it into a whole way of life.

Musicians know things like this. Of course, anyone who watches TV does too. You don't see many shows on the lives of unnoticed people, do you? It doesn't make good entertainment. But just mention names like Michael Jordan, Britney Spears, Johnny Depp, or Shania Twain, and everybody tunes in. With the onslaught of reality shows, it's not even just about fame anymore—it's about *instant* fame.

There's a big problem with fame, of course. Any brush with being famous really does a number on the human brain. A song by one of my favorites, Brad Paisley, sums it up. The chorus says:

When you're a celebrity
It's adios reality
You can act just like a fool
And people think you're cool
Just cause you're on TV…

It's a tongue-in-cheek song, but oh so true. For some reason, being famous in our culture catapults you into an unrealistic world. A ridiculous world, actually. People are waiting at every turn to serve you, do your hair, carry your bags, drive your car, excuse your disgusting behavior, clean up after you…

You have to ask, What would Jesus do with the whole "I am famous" thing?

I did. And it got me thinking.

HE IS THE FAMOUS ONE

Have you ever considered that Jesus *was* a rather famous person in His day?

The Bible says that everywhere He went large crowds followed. But look who was in those crowds. No crew from *Entertainment Tonight* in sight. Just ordinary folks lined up to see Him, sometimes by the thousands. Jesus' crowds tended to be made up of the hurting, the discouraged, the ill and weak and handicapped and wayward and forgotten.

(You have to love His fan base.) All of them longed to get close to Him, to touch Him, to hear Jesus say those words of life (it's what all of us ragamuffins still want today).

Of course, Jesus' real fame is still to come. The Bible says that,

> God exalted him to the highest place and gave him the name that is above every name, that at the name of Jesus every knee should bow…and every tongue confess that Jesus Christ is Lord, to the glory of God the Father. (Philippians 2:9–11)

That's fame beyond our wildest imagination. Every person who has breath will declare Jesus as Lord and King, the Bible says. That's all 6.5 billion (give or take a few) on this planet right now, plus everyone who has lived before us and will live after us.

So think of Jesus in a new light—as the supreme celebrity, the one who should be—and will be—getting all the admiration, all the attention, all the service, and all the praise.

A few years ago I realized I wanted to write a song about the fame of Jesus. Why not? He's the famous One. And His fame matters—a lot! As His followers, you and I are called to build His fame in every way possible.

People today don't always understand Christian words like *glorify* or *holy* or *worship* or *praise*. But everyone knows exactly what you mean when you say *famous*. And even though *famous* isn't a word you'll hear a lot in a Sunday worship service, I thought it could give both churched and nonchurched people a fresh perspective on God's true splendor and renown.

That desire is at the heart of the chorus of "Famous One":

You are the Lord
the famous One,
the famous One
Great is your name in all the earth
The Heavens declare
You're glorious, glorious
Great is your fame beyond the earth

Even when the song was done, I had no idea if other worshipers would really connect with it. But "Famous One" seems to have struck a powerful chord, maybe because all of us struggle with the fame thing. I don't mean how you should feel about those TV cameras on your front lawn—most of us will never have to deal with that. It's much closer to the bone. Like, who should be at the center of your life?

Who should be getting all your attention—you or Jesus?

We all have a ferocious inborn desire to hog the spotlight in our own life. We express this desire in different ways. Shy people may not want to stand front and center. But by nature they're no less driven to get affirmation and attention. Hey, we all want our world to revolve around us...*somehow*.

But our new life in Christ calls us to something radically different and better—to make Jesus, and only Him, famous in our life.

"Famous One"—and in fact the whole *Not to Us* album—tackles this tug-of-war head-on. It's a constant battle for me. My insatiable human desires continually want more and more. But the Spirit of God at work in me continually shows that what I really need is less and less of Chris and more and more of Christ.

If you and I can't settle this struggle for the spotlight, it's "adios, reality." We'll end up living out a warped, self-centered, worship-deprived faith. Because you and I were *not* created for our own fame. We were created to give it all to God and to put ourselves in the background.

That brings me to another tricky word.

HUMILITY, THE OTHER SIDE OF FAME

Once we decide to live for God's fame alone, it's natural for us to ask, "Well, what would that kind of radically

God-centered life look like on an everyday basis?"

Jesus came to earth to give us the answer to that one too. Look again at the passage in Philippians 2. Here, Paul shows believers the direct link between Jesus' never-been-matched fame ("equality with God") and His surprising lifestyle ("he humbled himself"). Paul wrote:

> Your attitude should be the same as that of Christ Jesus: Who, being in very nature God, did not consider equality with God something to be grasped, but made himself nothing, taking the very nature of a servant, being made in human likeness. And being found in appearance as a man, he humbled himself and became obedient to death—even death on a cross! (vv. 5–8)

Think about those words: "Being in very nature God…made himself nothing." How is that even possible? To be King over all created things (from the dust you're standing on to the star at the farthest edge of the farthest galaxy), to be stronger than any being or force or obstacle in the universe, to be all-good, all-knowing, all-loving…and then to choose to be nothing? To choose a criminal's death? For me? For you?

That's *humility*! And here's the thing—if complete

humility before God the Father was Christ's chosen life-style, then it has to be ours too.

When people ask what I think is the most important characteristic of a life of worship, I can't ever get past that word. *Humility.* I just don't see how you can truly worship God until you really *know* how famous He is (and realize how *not* famous you are).

CHAMPIONS OF THE UNNOTICED LIFE

What picture comes to your mind when you think about what it means to be humble? Honestly, my first take is to imagine a soft-spoken, plain-dressed, wallflower of a person who drives a junker. He (or she) is probably boring too. Yep, for some reason that's the epitome of humility to me.

But why? Probably because I tend to look on the outside. But God looks inside, because humility is a state of the heart. Humility is a holy attitude. Sure, you and I can be fooled by false humility for a while, but only a while. A person's real attitude surfaces sooner or later. I've encountered genuine humility in both the wealthiest of people and in the poorest. Maybe you have too.

Here's a word picture that helps me understand humility: *A humble person is a champion of the unnoticed life.*

Sounds weak, I know. Definitely not worth a TV show. But champions of the unnoticed life have enormous power. These men and women influence their world without ever seeming to be in the spotlight. That place of attention and honor has been rightly given over to Someone Else.

Let me introduce you to some of the champions who've had a huge influence in my life:

"Where are the most expensive cigarettes?"— Neil's story

Neil is one of those guys that can read your mail, if you know what I mean. He sees through to the truth about people and situations and seems to know what to do. All in a very unnoticed kind of way. I could tell you four or five stories that would blow you away, but I'll keep it to one.

Neil was having lunch at the Kettle (yep, the same landmark of Brownwood cuisine I already mentioned). He was in the area for a speaking engagement. Neil loves places like the Kettle and Waffle House. He says that's where Jesus would eat.

Well, the waitress had walked up to take his order when Neil noticed she seemed worn out. Their conversation went something like this:

Neil: "How are ya?"

Waitress: "I'm really tired. Been working two jobs to

make ends meet. And I'm just waiting for my fifteen-minute break."

Neil: "What are you going to do on your break?"

Waitress: "Oh, grab a smoke. I can't wait."

Neil: "What kind of cigarettes you smoke?"

Waitress, looking a little surprised: "Ah, the generic ones. Can't afford the expensive ones. What would you like to eat?"

Neil ordered.

Neil ate.

Neil paid.

Then Neil went straight to the nearest Wal-Mart. "Say," he said to the first employee he met, "I'm here to buy your most expensive cigarettes. Can you help me?" (He didn't have a lot of experience in this particular kind of shopping.)

As soon as he made his purchase, Neil headed back to the Kettle. His timing couldn't have been more perfect. When he pulled up, a cluster of waitresses were out back on break, his waitress among them. They stood near the trash bin, passing one lit cigarette around for all to share.

Neil headed toward them with the expensive stuff. (He told me later they looked at him like he was Ed McMahon driving up in the Publishers Clearing House van.) He handed the cigarettes to the woman who had waited on him. "I just want you to know that God cares about you just the way you are," he said. "Enjoy these."

He was starting back to his car when the waitress said, "Sir?"

"Yeah?"

"Are you a preacher in this town?"

"No," Neil replied. "Just speaking at a church here for a few nights. Then I'm moving on."

"That's too bad," said the waitress. She was still holding the cigarettes like some kind of grand prize. Neil noticed she was tearing up.

"Too bad," she repeated, her voice trembling, "'cause I would like to go to your church."

I love that story! The waitress never knew Neil's name, but when he left, she knew that God cared about her. That's what an unnoticed life looks like, I think. A person who humbly makes God's fame great to others in a language they understand.

And what an accomplishment! Why wouldn't that be worth the finest pack of smokes a guy could buy?

"Lord, make me obscure"—J. D.'s story

J. D. is another one of those special people. His example in my life shows me the power of dying to my own importance and reputation and taking the way of Jesus. It probably helps that J. D. grew up on a farm (in Arkansas). Farms tend to produce good food *and* good people. J. D. is one of them. I first noticed it when we wrote a couple of songs together.

We didn't think too much about it at the time, but when the songs started getting picked up for recording by several artists, we had to deal with the paperwork. For example, we needed to sign contracts protecting our ownership and any royalty payments that might come our way. But when we sat down to do that, J. D. signed over all his earnings to ministries that help widows and orphans.

As it has turned out, the songs have gotten more popular and the earnings checks fatter, and for three years they've stayed that way. But J. D. has stuck with his personal giveaway plan.

That's living an unnoticed life for God's fame.

Oh, J. D.'s had plenty of chances to make a name for himself. He graduated from law school near the top of his class, then went off to Washington to be the next senator from Arkansas. And he was well on his way to that goal. But God grabbed his attention and whispered to his heart that he could change his world more effectively through a surrendered life than a celebrated one. Now he's in full-time ministry—dean of students at a major seminary.

J. D.'s most recent idea was to start a fellowship of anonymous songwriters. He calls their work "hidden songs." All royalties go to ministries for the poor.

The lyrics of the first "hidden" song get the point across better than anything I could say:

Lord, make me obscure
Keep me unnoticed
Let me be known by Your image in me
Broken by grace and mended by mercy
Let me be hidden
Hidden in You
Hidden in the rock behind Your glory
Hidden in the cross beneath Your shame
Let me be as lost inside Your greatness
To be found within Your name
Let me be lost in You
Till I am found in You
Let me be hidden
Hidden in You

That's J. D. He's living out the gospel in unseen ways. (Keep it up, my friend. You're a champion to me.)

There are two more champions of God's fame I'd like you to meet. They're already part of Tomlin family legend…

First to serve, last to eat—
Grandma Tomlin's story

I wish I could write a whole book about my Grandmother Tomlin—or Mamaw. You see, I just got back home from her funeral this weekend. It's so strange that I would be thinking about her life for this book and attending her funeral at the same time.

Margurie Tomlin was an amazing woman. She had no earthly possessions to speak of. In fact, she would be considered poor by most standards. But she left behind a rich legacy that will bless her descendants for generations. I'll never forget our Thanksgiving and Christmas family feasts at her house, the wonderful aromas that filled her home when we walked in—of oven-roasted turkey and dressing, southern fried chicken, freshly baked rolls, sweet potato casserole, broccoli and cheese casserole, and apple pie.

Oh, and the best chocolate cake you ever laid a fork to!

Mamaw walked everywhere she needed to go—never had a driver's license. "If you drive," she used to say, "you have to always look at the road. But when I walk, I can look at everything."

She was a charter member of the little Baptist church in her hometown, and she loved the Lord with all her heart and strength. She especially loved to sing the songs of the faith. She was always asking me to play her favorites, like

"Because He Lives" and "How Great Thou Art." Come Christmas you could count on her to pipe up with a request for "O Come, All Ye Faithful."

I guess we live in a take-all-you-can-get world, but Mamaw's was more like a give-all-you-can-give world. It was a better place. Thinking back, I can't say I recall seeing her actually sit down to eat during those holiday feasts. I just remember Mamaw bustling around, making sure everyone else was happy and well fed. Sure, she'd take a nibble here and there. But before my brothers and I could swallow our second mouthful, she was already asking if we wanted more. That kind of love can change a boy.

She wasn't suffering in her service. Not in the least! She was simply living out her dearest pleasure—to serve the ones she loved in Jesus' name.

As we sat in that church to remember Margurie Tomlin a few days ago, I thought a lot about her generosity to all of us. What a quiet, sweet lady she was! "Full of class and grace," my cousin eulogized. *Yes!* I thought, as I looked around and saw the family she had loved and served and prayed for so tirelessly.

The thing about an unnoticed life, you know, is that you rarely see the power of it while it's happening. You have to wait—maybe until eternity. But this weekend I was reminded of how much one humble life can give to the world. I saw Mamaw's gift in the faces all around me. I came home carrying it in my heart.

In the past few days, I've been thinking a lot on Jesus' words that one day the first will be last and the last will be first.

Well, Mamaw is first now.

Faithful in little things— Grandpa Duncan's story

Everybody has a hero in their life. Mine is my Grandfather Duncan, or Papaw, as I liked to call him. I've always looked up to him. All through my boyhood, I hung on his every word. I even listened to every word when he prayed before a meal.

Papaw reminded us often to be thankful for what God had given us. Being that he was part of the Great Depression generation, he had a good perspective on thankfulness. Back then, he told us, Christmas was different. Christmas morning he'd get an apple and a toothbrush. That was it— and the toothbrush had to last till the next Christmas.

My brothers and I loved to spend our summers with Papaw and Grandma Noni at their house on the lake. Every morning, Papaw would wake me up before sunrise, and we'd head out on the water in search of lunch and dinner. I loved fishing with him. And waterskiing too.

But I especially remember taking a drive with him one afternoon. We were rattling down some back roads when he stopped the truck. "I want you to know where you come from," he said. He pointed out my side window. There wasn't much to look at there, just a dusty field. But Papaw explained that this was the place where his parents had been sharecroppers and where he'd grown up.

He drove farther, to the end of the road. "This is where I first saw your grandmother," he said. "I thought she was shining and lovely." He said he decided on the spot that he had to figure out how to meet her, and I guess he succeeded.

The next stop on our little drive took us to another empty space beside the road. "The church our family attends started right here many years ago," he said. Papaw pointed to a beautiful oak tree. "I was standing right about where that tree is when I asked Jesus to save me," he said. "It was the most important decision of my life." Just the way he said it, I could tell that his salvation experience was as real and amazing to him then as it had been on the first day.

A truck ride like that can change a boy too. I was so proud that afternoon to be riding with my papaw, and I've been blessed to go through life with his example to inspire me. He's the most faithful man I know. Every Sunday morning, he teaches a Bible study for his church. It's the same Bible study he was teaching when I was five.

I want to be like that. I want to look back and say, "I have been faithful in the little things." That would be a worthy unnoticed life for the glory of God.

THE JOURNEY AWAY
FROM THE SPOTLIGHT

In the previous chapter, we looked at who our awesome God is and why we should respond to Him with a lifetime of worship and service. In this chapter, I took you on a trail of evidence that began in the glare of the spotlights and ended up beside a country road.

Think of it as a progression of ideas intended to take you further and further from seeking attention for yourself, and closer and closer to crowning Jesus as the only famous One, the only King of Glory in your life.

Where would you put yourself in this journey away from the spotlight and toward an unnoticed life?

Listen, choosing to make God (not yourself) famous in your life can be a turning point. I'll be the first to admit that the unnoticed life—of humility, obedience, and putting God first—doesn't have much sex appeal. The choice never gets easier. It's death—death to every molecule of you that rises for attention and notice. But it's also a birth into God's amazing upside-down kingdom.

And it can be a lot of fun. Some days it'll make you laugh out loud with surprise and joy.

Which leads me to my last story.

WHAT THE T-SHIRT SAID

The apartments where I live have a workout area in the basement. One Monday afternoon in December, I was down there sweating it out on the treadmill. The TV happened to be tuned to the VH1 Music Awards show, and somebody introduced Shania Twain.

Well, that got my attention. Not for the obvious reason that Shania is gorgeous, but because a friend from Chicago, Roddy Chiong, plays fiddle (and a lot of other instruments) in her band.

Shania and her guys took the stage and, sure enough, there was Roddy, in front of millions on TV, playing for one of the premier entertainers of our time. But that wasn't even the best part. The best part was Roddy's T-shirt.

Now let me tell you about that…

I have to take you back to 3:00 one morning. My bass player Jesse is driving back to Austin from somewhere else in Texas. It's not a safe time of night for him or me when Jesse's out late because he comes up with most of his really brilliant ideas when he's sleep deprived. Then he has to call and wake me up. That's what he does. I'm still fumbling in the dark with the phone when Jesse starts talking.

"Hey, I've got a great idea for a T-shirt," he yells, all fired up. Right off, that doesn't strike me as the best news to be waked from a dead sleep for. Besides, we've never been much of a T-shirt band. But Jesse is convinced. "We've always wanted something that really made a statement, you know? Well, I've got the statement. What would you think about a simple star on the front of a shirt, with 'I am not famous' written across it?"

I must admit, I loved it. The design and message of that T-shirt could go perfectly with our music.

So for the next Passion Tour, we took a big risk and ordered a truckload of shirts. People loved the "I am not famous" shirt so much that we couldn't keep that crazy thing in stock (I think we reordered four times on the tour).

Now back to the VH1 Music Awards show…

Maybe you guessed it—there's Roddy standing next to Shania, fiddling his heart out and wearing his "I am not famous" shirt onstage. In the middle of Glam Central. In the middle of Shania's song, for crying out loud! (And I could have sworn the cameraman kept his lens on Roddy for most of the song.)

Way to go, Roddy! Thanks for standing in the spotlight and humbly spreading the message of the famous One.

I WANT TO LOOK BACK AND SAY,
"I HAVE BEEN FAITHFUL IN THE LITTLE THINGS."
THAT WOULD BE A WORTHY UNNOTICED LIFE
FOR THE GLORY OF GOD.

top: Traveling in Africa with Passion.
Louie's wife, Shelley, is also my manager.
above: Daniel and I making a joyful noise.

CHAPTER FIVE

THE NOISE WE MAKE

D id you know that disagreements over music styles split more churches today than any other issue?

Kind of depressing, I think. But while folks left and right are arguing about what we should sing and how and whether or not someone should pull the plug on the amps, I think it might be more useful to ask, "Does the Bible have anything to say about worship styles?"

That's what I want to look at in the next few pages.

You wouldn't think that how we praise God in or out of church would get people so heated up. But it does. I learned that lesson on the very first concert I booked that came complete with an airline ticket.

I couldn't believe it. Here I was still in college, and someone was willing to fly me, my guitar, and my drum machine somewhere just so I could play. Wow!

My destination: Talladega, Alabama.

Sound Check

Everything seemed all right when I landed. The youth pastor who picked me up at the airport said they were expecting about five hundred people to come to the concert. Five hundred people would make it my biggest audience ever.

But things quickly started going south. I was getting ready for sound check at the church when I was introduced to my sound engineer for the night. She was fourteen. I had to explain to her that faders on a mixing board mean volume. It wasn't too long before I politely took over and began getting the sound ready myself. I guess she wandered off home.

Problem was that the sound board was in the balcony. I'd strum my guitar, listen for a minute, then run upstairs and adjust. This process took me about two hours, but at least it burned up a lot of nervous energy.

I was just about finished and close to liking it when an older gentleman entered from the back of the auditorium. I could see him pounding his ears with his hands and yelling at me. But I was still getting the sound adjusted, so I couldn't make out what he was saying. To fix that, he ran up to the balcony and turned two hours worth of micro-adjusting down to zero.

Who is this guy? I wondered, my heart sinking. *And what does he think he's doing?*

|

Well, he had an answer. "Young man!" he bellowed from the balcony, "I'm the music minister of this church, and I will not have this kind of music played in my sanctuary! You're way too loud! You're going to ruin everybody's ears!" (Notice the exclamation points.)

I stood there like a deer in the headlights. I couldn't believe what was happening. And I didn't know what to say.

He announced that he'd be running the sound for the concert. *Well,* I thought, *we're really going to rock Talladega tonight.*

The next ten minutes went something like this:

"What do you need?" he yelled down from the balcony.

"I'm going to need some volume on the acoustic guitar," I said.

"No you don't!" he yelled. "That's why it's 'acoustic.' Don't need to plug it in. What else do you need?"

"Uh, how about my drum machine?"

"I don't like drums," he yelled, almost cheerfully. "Don't think they should be used in this church." Then he turned helpful. "I'll give you a little microphone, though!" he shouted, reaching for a control and giving it a tiny nudge.

I tested it. "Could I have a little more?"

Another nudge.

"Thanks. Say, could I have a little more?"

And another.

On a scale of ten, we finally had the PA up to about three.

Finally the music minister descended from the balcony to talk. He put his hands on my shoulders and looked me in the eyes. "Young man," he said, "God has put me here to be a steward of the human ear. I'm fifty-five years old, and I still have good hearing because I've never listened to music like you play. You are going to ruin these kids' ears and yours as well. You are not being a good steward of the human ear."

Steward of the human ear? Never heard it said quite like that before. It was all I could do to keep from saying, "Huh? What?"

And to think I was only at sound check.

By now another problem had gotten my attention. It was 6:55, the concert started at 7:00, and there was no one else in the room but me and the ear steward. I mean, *no* one.

I went looking for the youth minister. "Hey, if five hundred people are coming, they must all be coming in one car," I said, unable to hide my slight concern. That's when he let it slip that actually he didn't know if anyone was coming. A lot was going on downtown, he said. But not to worry—he had made some calls and thought a few warm bodies might show up anytime.

Back in the auditorium, I discovered he was right. We

had seven warm bodies, probably all his relatives, and they didn't look happy to be there. Talk about humbling.

Just when I was about to start anyway, another group of people started filtering in from the back. This was a much larger group, maybe about thirty. But something seemed a little different about them. When I asked the youth pastor, he said, "Oh yeah. I called the blind and deaf school and had them bused over. Thought that they might fill up some seats."

So this is what I got for my first complete-with-airfare gig:

- 7 people who would rather be anywhere but there
- 30 folks who either couldn't hear me or couldn't see me
- 1 overachieving youth pastor, and
- 1 fiftysomething steward of the human ear.

You know, sometimes you just gotta stand up and play. And that's what I did in Talladega. Honestly, I don't remember much about the actual concert part of the evening. I think it went all right. I remember it as quiet. Yeah, that's what it was. *Real* quiet.

I laughed the entire flight home.

Breaking the Sound Barrier

Look at it this way: The arguments about worship styles are just more proof that God wired each of us uniquely. Because of our uniqueness, we respond differently to almost everything. Why shouldn't our worship responses to God be different as well? To put preferences in a box and say, "Only what's in this box gets to be the look and sound of worship" would be wrong.

I have some friends who are just expressionless. When they get excited, you might see an eyebrow twitch. For them getting rowdy sounds like one bored fan clapping for a no-name golfer who just made a bogey. But I've learned these friends really are full of joy. They just express it differently. (Maybe the senior warden of human ears in Talladega was one of these guys—who am I to say?) So I've learned not to judge what's going on in someone's soul by what's going on in their outward appearance.

That said, the Bible *does* have some things to say about how we should worship. And these responses of worship should supersede all our personalities and preferences. The reason is simple—we don't find these responses in Scripture as suggestions but as *commands*.

Let's look at some:

Lift your hands. The Bible actually implores us to lift up our hands to God in worship. Psalm 134:2 says, "Lift up your hands in the sanctuary and praise the LORD." Why? I think raising our hands to God communicates so many different, important things.

Like many, I grew up in a church that was quite conservative. You only raised your hand if you had a question (and you didn't get to have those in church), so I had to *learn* to raise my hands.

Which is odd when you think about it. Raised hands are so rich with meaning.

Watch any football game on Sunday afternoon, or any sport for that matter. When an athlete scores or pulls off something heroic on the field, what is the immediate response? Hands shoot up! It's the natural sign that someone has won and you're extremely happy about it. You don't have to think. You just reach for the sky!

Or you're watching an episode of *COPS*. The police finally collar the shirtless drunk. He sees what's about to go down—and up go his hands! Right? To raise the hands in that situation is a wise move (probably his first in weeks). It's the universal sign of surrender. How much more in worship do we express our joy in surrender to Jesus and His lordship of our lives?

One last example: Just watch a small child when Mom or Dad comes home after being gone all day. Up go the chubby little hands! The child is saying, "Please pick me up and hold me! I'm so happy to see you!" How much more is our joy to hold out our arms for our Father to pick us up, to hold us in His eternal arms?

You see it at rock or country music concerts all the time—people reaching, pleading, waving, hoping with outstretched hands toward the star onstage. These fans would give anything for just a touch from their favorite star. But sadly, the star onstage doesn't have much to give in return for all that desire. A song and a good time maybe. But our famous God has everything to give. He holds out *life* for the taking. How much more should we lift up our hands to Him?

Bow down. Psalm 95:6 says, "Come, let us bow down in worship, let us kneel before the LORD our Maker." What a beautiful picture of expressing subordination and respect. We just don't worship someone we think we're bigger or more important than. That's why bowing is the right position for us before almighty God.

In John 4, Jesus is talking to the woman at the well about worship. He tells her, "A time is coming when you will worship the Father neither on this mountain nor in Jerusalem" (v. 21). The translation of that word *worship* Jesus uses means to literally "bow down and kiss the feet of a king." Wow!

If you're like me, you've lived in the United States all your life and don't have much perspective on relating to a king or queen as a ruler. Americans don't even bow before our president, so most of us have never had a good model of this behavior. But consider your position before the Lord. When was the last time you bowed your face to the ground in adoration of and reverence for Him? I don't mean a little nod in the right direction. And I don't mean bowing your head in prayer. I mean face and body down—in complete, reverential surrender before Him.

Sometimes while I'm leading others in a worship song, I'll feel suddenly overcome with the realization of who it is we're singing to, of how great is our king, and of how small and unworthy I am to make even a sound in His presence! At those times I often find myself on my knees. Not for show, God forbid, but because the truth takes me down to size. I'm just the guy with the guitar. But He is the Lord— the Lord of lords, the King of kings, the God above all gods!

To bow in His presence is only right.

Be still before Him. Ecclesiastes 5:2: "Do not be quick with your mouth, do not be hasty in your heart to utter anything before God. God is in heaven and you are on earth, so let your words be few." Verse 7: "Much dreaming and many words are meaningless. Therefore stand in awe of God."

How many times do we just flippantly walk into a worship service and begin singing or praying with little thought beforehand. I've always thought church would be much better if people came to bring their offerings, to give their thanks, to celebrate God's faithfulness, to praise Him for His provision...and pretty much shut up about everything else. That's the church I want to be a part of—the one that enters ready to meet with God.

None of this happens without stillness and quietness of soul. Our world is so loud. TV, Internet, radio, iPods, traffic, cell phones, Muzak, intercoms, and the list goes on. I think this constant volume of nothingness pushes us farther and farther from people. It's like the sounds become a barrier or wall between us and our surroundings.

We don't really know how to be quiet. But how do we expect to hear anything from God in all the noise? When was the last time you quieted your world and just stood in awe of God?

From time to time, I'll lead a group in a time of silence. For some people, it's awkward. When you're up front you can feel the worry waves—*How long will this go on? Hope I don't sneeze. I must look dumb just standing here...* I guess even in church we don't know how to slow down and listen. Our services and Christian events are filled with noise. We're afraid of a dead space in the program. We're afraid of silence.

I remember finishing the song "Shout to the Lord" and just letting it breathe with the people for a moment—no music, just letting the thought of what we had sung sink into the heart, soul, and mind of the congregation. It was a powerful moment. Afterward an older gentleman approached me to say that he had noticed when I forgot what song came after "Shout to the Lord." I told him politely that, actually, the silence was intentional.

Our silence before God should be intentional.

Shout for joy! Now to the opposite response—making *a lot* of noise! I love these verses from the Psalms: "Let us shout aloud to the Rock of our salvation" (95:1), and "Shout for joy to the LORD, all the earth" (100:1). Over and over, the Psalms picture all of creation making a lot of noise in praise of God. And it's a worship celebration that's going on *all* the time!

Personally, shouting as an act of worship is a stretch for me. I just don't shout about many things. But I do know there have been times when I couldn't keep something wonderful inside. Hopefully you know the feeling too. It happened to me in high school when Tammy said yes.

I was a freshman, stood about five feet tall, and weighed about a dollar. Tammy was a senior, a baton twirler, and the prettiest girl I'd ever seen. I still can't believe I was crazy enough to ask her out, but I did. When I asked her out for pizza, she said yes. Even when I told her I couldn't drive, she said yes. Yes, she'd go out with me, and yes, she'd come by Saturday night and pick me up!

When I hung up the phone, I started running and shouting. I could hear the "Hallelujah Chorus" coming from the heavens. I shouted up the hall, then I shouted down. I called every guy I knew and hit him with the news—Tammy had said yes! And I just had to make a lot of noise about it.

Incredible joy can make you behave that way. And honest worship should sometimes too.

I remember a surprise God had for me as a worship leader in Malaysia. I was expecting a quiet service; after all, the Malaysian church has suffered much persecution. But between songs, the pastor leaned over and said, "God likes a noisy church. We want a noisy church. Let's sing 'The Noise We Make.'"

So we cranked it up. About thirty seconds in, everybody in the room brought out whistles—I'm not kidding—and began to make as much noise as possible. I'd never heard that much whistling in one place before. I couldn't hear the band. I couldn't hear me. Just an incredible, roof-raising celebration of God. It was great!

I wonder if the early church sounded anything like that? I like to think so. (Okay, maybe minus the whistles, but definitely all of the passion.) Like Malaysian Christians, the early church followed Jesus at risk to their safety, reputation, possessions—even their lives. In the midst of so much opposition, God was truly their joy. A God like that calls for a *lot* of noise.

Even dance. The Bible says there is a time to dance (Ecclesiastes 3:4). Is worship one of them? Give it some thought.

You might remember the Old Testament story where David celebrates the return of the ark of the covenant (the symbol of God's presence) to Jerusalem. Here's what David did:

> David, wearing a linen ephod, danced before the LORD with all his might, while he and the entire house of Israel brought up the ark of the LORD with shouts and the sound of trumpets. (2 Samuel 6:14–15)

David was so grateful for what God was doing that he couldn't *not* move. He had to dance. And he didn't just sway or shuffle politely. He danced "before the LORD with all his might." Even when his wife, Michal, scolded him later for embarrassing her in public, David was defiant. "I will celebrate before the LORD," he said. "I will become even more undignified than this" (vv. 21–22).

That is the heart of a worshiper! Even though David was king, he was ready to humble himself in public to make God great.

Of course, we don't know how *well* David danced. But then again, maybe we do. He embarrassed his wife (there's a clue).

But of course, worshiping through dance isn't about having smooth moves or a great sense of rhythm. It's not about how we look at all. Dancing before God is about our heart.

To be honest, many days I'm a long way from that kind of freedom in my worship. I want to keep my status. I'd rather people think I'm cool. But those human desires can get in the way of full expression in worship. Truth is, there's nothing about looking cool and worshiping Jesus that go together. However you sing it, shout it, bow it, or dance it, it's not a cool thing in our world to give full-on applause and glory to God. You might just be returning thanks for your food at a burger joint. But when you honor God in public, you *will* risk looking uncool.

Worship calls for that kind of abandonment to the full joy of God's presence. And when I look out onto a crowd of true worshipers, that's what I love to see. Not folks who are making sure they have the right stance or their hair is perfect. I'm looking for the Davids—the folks who are willing to put aside what the person next to them might think and simply express to God just how thankful they are to be in His presence.

"PULA! PULA! PULA!"

One night when our team was ministering in Botswana, in southern Africa, word spread that the village chief was coming to attend the service. Immediately we sensed both excitement and anxiety in the audience.

Sure enough, in the middle of a song, the chief made his entrance. Suddenly, the music stopped and the crowd parted down the middle to make a way for him to get to the front. As he walked forward his people thrust their hands in the air and began to shout, *"Pula! Pula! Pula!"*

What did that shout mean? I wondered. (*Could it mean "Kill the white man"?*) A little apprehensive, I looked down our row of very white faces.

Fortunately, the missionary sitting with us saw my worry and explained. *Pula*, he said, was the most precious word in their language. It was the word they used for *money*, for *rain*, and for *highest honor*—all three. Any time the chief entered a public gathering, it was their custom to offer him their highest praise and honor by shouting their most precious word…

"Pula! Pula! Pula!"

After the chief had given the crowd his greeting, he took a seat, and the African worship leader thanked him for stopping by. Then he told the audience it was time to get back to the reason we had gathered. We were here to worship the *kosi ana kosi*, the Chief of chiefs. At that, the crowd began to throw their fists in the air again and shout, "*Pula! Pula! Pula!*" even louder.

That was an awakening moment for me. What if we really believed that the Chief of chiefs walked into every worship service? I grabbed a pen and as fast as I could write, these words came out:

You set my feet to dancing
You set my heart on fire
In the presence of a thousand kings
You are my one desire
And I stand before you now
With trembling hands lifted high
Be glorified…

A GENERATION IN MOTION

Here's the most important thing to remember about worship styles: When it comes to music and singing songs of worship to God, it's ultimately not about loud or quiet. It's not about how many folks show up. It's not about amplified or acoustic, contemporary or traditional. It's not about what you do with your hands or your feet.

Worship is still about *Jesus*. He is the Chief of chiefs and Lord above all. And if you make Him *your* Lord, then you're ready to respond "in spirit and in truth." And however you express it, true worship will always set you in motion toward the object of your affection—God Himself.

Because that's the way you were made!

Since our outward expressions are many times a picture of our heart, let me ask you—what does your heart look like at the moment? Are you ready to declare—and show—the same longing of the Israelites who said, "Your name and your renown are the desire of our souls" (Isaiah 26:8)?

Join me and so many others in this young, emerging church of Jesus worshipers. Join us as we throw open our arms and throw back our heads to shout and dance and exult in honor of our King.

Sure, there's likely to be a self-appointed "steward of the human ear" watching. God love 'em—maybe they just need something to do on a quiet afternoon in Talladega. Or wherever you are.

And maybe it's your job to give it to them.

top left: With my brothers,
Ryan (left) and Cory (right)
above: Worshiping with a
great crowd at OneDay '03

CHAPTER SIX

SPIRIT OVERFLOW

I love playing at summer camps and festivals. The people really get into it. Even if you can't see them too well in the glare of the spotlights, you sure can hear them.

Like one time last summer. We were playing "Famous One" to a full arena. Everyone really started screaming. I thought, *Man, they really want to worship!*

Then I noticed that the screams weren't coming at the right places in the song. So I stepped back out of the glare of the lights to see what was happening. Thousands of kids had a wave going around the stadium, and they were really having a good time.

For a second the people pleaser in me thought I should just let it go—make sure everyone had fun and liked me for it. But I couldn't. We stopped the song, and the band just stood there. Of course, the wave kept rolling, along with the screams, around and around. It took a while for the kids to notice we weren't playing.

When the place finally settled down, I stepped to the mic and said, "I want you to have a good time and like our music. But that's not what's most important to me. I don't see how you can sing this song and be doing the wave. Do you have any idea what you're singing?"

By then the whole arena was deathly quiet. I sure had their attention.

"This song is all about God," I continued, trying to be gentle. "But what you're doing is bringing all the attention to yourselves. You can do the wave all you want when our band is offstage. But when we're playing, we want to make all our music, all our words, and all our joy about God and His glory. That's the only reason we're here!"

More deathly quiet.

Then the crowd burst out in applause and cheering (really, most kids there *did* want to focus on God). When we started up "Famous" again, everyone was on the same page and things went much better.

WHEN IT'S TIME TO LEAD

Taking control like that—stepping in with a hard word when folks were having so much fun—was *so* hard on me! I'm a cheerleader, not a policeman, by nature. But I wasn't up on that stage just to make music or to be popular. I was there to lead worship. Being a worship leader means I deeply desire to use the gifts God has given me to lead others in a meaningful response to Him. That's my ministry. And for ministry to happen in group situations, somebody usually has to step out and lead.

That's what I want to look at in this chapter.

You may not be on a church payroll as a worship leader. But you're probably active in families, small groups, Bible studies, or with Christian friends where worship occurs. You can be ready to lead in those situations too. The truth is, we're *all* called to be worship ministers—to lift up the name of Jesus every day, and to live in such a way that we help others do the same.

But in this chapter I'm also thinking of those who feel specifically gifted and called to lead through music. Are you one? If so, then you face tough questions like:

- How do you prepare well—and deliver well—for the best worship experience possible?
- How much does the leader make worship happen, and how much is up to the Spirit?
- How important is it to keep the congregation happy with your music selections or style?

- What's the best way for the worship leader to work well with the lead pastor?

Just for a moment, think back to my motley audience in Talladega (previous chapter). Remember?

Some blind.

Some deaf.

Some sincerely motivated.

Some sincerely wishing they were somewhere else...

You know, *Sunday services all around the country are a lot like that!* Every audience is full of people who are resisting a worship experience for all kinds of reasons. They may be tired. They may dislike the pastor. They may feel angry at God or wonder if they still believe in Him. They may be spiritually numbed by sin. They may be suffering in a relationship. They may be in deep financial trouble. The list could go on.

But that's reality. And that's where leadership is tested.

So if we're called to minister through music, where should we start?

Jesus told us. He said, "God is spirit, and his worshipers must worship in spirit and in truth" (John 4:24). Not a word about style, or acoustics, or the color of the carpet. Not a word about the motley audience...

We simply start with the Spirit.

THE HOLY SPIRIT AS LEAD WORSHIPER

The Holy Spirit is the ultimate lead worshiper of the church. Jesus told His disciples, "When the Counselor comes, whom I will send to you from the Father, the Spirit of truth who goes out from the Father, he will testify about me" (John 15:26). In many other passages, the New Testament shows us that we can count on the Holy Spirit to lead us as God's people into His presence.

Just knowing that the Holy Spirit is ultimately in charge can really lift the burden right off our shoulders. It's so easy to feel performance pressures, to carry the weight of what God is going (or not going) to do during the service. But that's not our burden to carry. That belongs to God's Spirit in our midst.

I was listening to Bono (lead singer of U2) one afternoon on *Oprah*. No, I don't usually watch the *The Oprah Winfrey Show,* but a friend had called and said that Bono would be on for an interview. Bono is a man I admire. Sure, he has his faults like anyone else, but he seems to have a bigger purpose than just to make a name for himself.

During their conversation, Oprah said she'd noticed that Bono was a very religious man. To which Bono (wearing his trademark blue shades) responded: "I don't consider myself religious. Religion is a lot like Elvis. When the Spirit leaves the building, you get religion. I'm just as comfortable in a Catholic church up north as I am in a tent meeting down South—if the Spirit is there. But if the Spirit isn't there, I'd rather not be in either place."

I agree. If the Spirit is not in the house, we should all just go home! It is the Spirit who leads us to God.

So why have I so often walked into a concert putting myself under huge pressure, thinking it's all up to me? As if God needed me to play perfectly, choose the perfect songs, and say all the right things before He—God of the universe—could make Himself known to anyone! As if anything delighted the Holy Spirit more than to make great the name of Jesus! Only in the last couple years have I been able to rest in the Spirit's leadership in any room where His people gather to worship. That takes a load off. And it should.

I'm thinking of a story in Matthew 16, where Jesus puts His boys on the spot. First He asks the disciples, "Who do people say the Son of Man is?" Then He turns and asks it more directly, "Who do *you* say I am?"

Peter speaks up and—for once—gets it right. "You are the Christ, the Son of the living God."

What Jesus says next turned on a lightbulb for me. I hope it does the same for you. Jesus told Peter, "Blessed are you...*for this was not revealed to you by man, but by my Father in heaven*" (vv. 13–17).

No individual—no matter how appealing or talented—can reveal the truth of God to another human soul. Only God can do that. That's why we must depend on the Spirit to come into our worship times in fullness and power.

"YOUR LIFE IS LIVING ME..."

Jesse and I were at his parents' ranch one evening. We had decided to get away for several hours and look through our songs and ask God if He had something else for us as well. Daniel, our brilliant guitar player, had given us his journal of lyrics to take with us for the night.

I was sitting at the ranch piano (which was badly out of tune, I might add), playing whatever came out. Jesse leafed through Daniel's journal entries, reading some aloud to me. Daniel isn't really one to speak up with song ideas. But it didn't take long for Jesse and I to feel that we'd been handed over a trunk filled with worship treasures.

One line grabbed us above the rest:

Your life is living me...

That sparked a lively discussion between Jesse and me about what a life of worship looks like. We decided that line said it so well—the life of God alive in each of us.

I recalled the prayer of a friend of mine: "Lord, may everything we do be just the overflow of You in our lives."

And that became the refrain of the song "Overflow."

THE SERVANT AS WORSHIP LEADER

Almost anyone can learn a few chords on a guitar and pick out their church's five favorite worship songs. But that doesn't mean they have been gifted and set aside to minister through music.

What's the difference?

Well, one might be that you can be a song leader without being a worship leader (one is about the music or the program; the other is about a Person). Another might be that you can be extremely talented musically—and put on absolutely dazzling shows—but not gifted or even motivated to lead believers to respond to God.

The worship leader's heart. I think it comes down to your heart. A true worship leader must have a heart that belongs completely to God. He or she is a servant who lives to know God better and bring Him more honor every day.

David the psalmist has to be my favorite example. I've proved that by basing so many of my songs on *his* songs. (When we get to heaven, I just know there's going to be a little "property rights" discussion over that!) Is there any body of worship material that is more loved and used today than the songs and prayers David wrote so many centuries ago? No, not even close. When David pours out his heart to God, we pour out ours too. That's worship leadership at its finest.

Take a few examples from the book of Psalms:

O LORD, our Lord, how majestic is your name in all the earth! (8:1)

And,

But I trust in your unfailing love;
    my heart rejoices in your salvation.
I will sing to the LORD,
    for he has been good to me. (13:5–6)

And,

I love you, O LORD, my strength.
    The LORD is my rock, my fortress and my deliverer;
my God is my rock, in whom I take refuge. (18:1–2)

And these examples are from just the first few pages of the book! If you're like me, you can recognize a familiar hymn, chorus, or worship song in almost every line.

Of course, David wasn't Mr. Perfect. But his heart, and all his hopes, belonged to God. He spent a lot of time listening to God, waiting on Him, talking to Him. David was slow to take the credit when things went well and quick to confess his sins when things didn't. From his writings it's clear that over his whole life, David pursued an honest friendship with God. I think it's because of that quality of relationship that David has been able to draw so many millions into worship along with him.

Do you think God gets fired up today about the latest hot young guitar player—the guy with the right clothes, the cool hair, and a great voice? Nah...and I don't think you think so either. Nothing wrong with any of those, but the worship leader God is after is the one whose heart is captured by Him.

The how-tos of this kind of life are actually pretty straight ahead. Take Ephesians 4–5, for example. Here we see Paul giving one of his rapid-fire lists of what living like a Christian looks like and its result:

- Live worthy of your calling
- Keep the unity of the Spirit
- Speak the truth in love
- Put off your old nature

- Put on the new nature
- Wake up
- Wise up
- Be filled with the Spirit...

And then what? Well, when you live like that, here's what happens:

> Then you will sing psalms and hymns and spiritual songs among yourselves, making music to the Lord in your hearts. And you will always give thanks for everything to God the Father in the name of our Lord Jesus Christ. (Ephesians 5:19–20, NLT)

Do you see how the response of worship is the natural result of a person's relationship with God? So the real impact of a worship leader's music starts inside him—in his heart, his motives, his walk with God.

From there a worship leader needs to know how to work well in a ministry team.

The worship leader's team. I've been blessed to minister in a team setting right from the start. To grow as an artist and minister, you need to be part of a group of people who share a vision and who are committed to your life. These are the people who can say things into your life in a way and at a time that will do the most good.

Like James Lankford, the evangelist I told you about. He really changed my life with this nugget—"Chris, you really don't know what you're doing up there, do you?"

I needed to hear that, and what came next—his anointing prayer that God would make me a psalm writer for my generation. Wow! You don't wake up the same person the next day when you're around people like that.

So I encourage you to look for a strong team, or ask God to help you build one. I absolutely treasure the people I've partnered with in some way in the past: Gregg Matte at Texas A&M, John David Walt at Woodlands United Methodist, Louie in the Passion ministry, and lately the pastoral team at the Austin Stone Community Church.

For my music ministry now, I have a small group of men and women who help me with decisions and hold me accountable. I need them, because being on the road a lot can be very disorienting. I remember one meeting with this group where they were helping me think through some challenges we were facing. As we talked and prayed together, a central theme rose up. And it was this: *Make men before music*. That was an important insight for me. Relationships, character, spiritual growth, faithfulness—all those internal things matter more than the externals of a busy life in music.

You can get so carried away with putting together your next service or catching your next flight that you completely lose sight of what you're here for in the first place.

Working in a team at church requires that we practice good communication, take good care of relationships, and do what it takes to build trust in each other. All of that takes time, humility, and pure motives. "Submit to one another out of reverence for Christ," Paul told the Ephesians (5:21).

Music, which has so much power to unite us in God's presence, should never be used to divide us as His people. I encourage you to work hard at team unity. Unity doesn't mean you never disagree. It means that you have one heart, you're going in the same direction, and you're on the same page about how you want to get there.

This kind of unity will never happen if you forget that the senior pastor is the most important worship leader in your church (after the Holy Spirit, of course). You may be the one with the guitar, but you are under authority. I know that some situations are less than desirable. Sometimes differences are too great to bridge. But it's a big mistake to think that you can take the church in your direction without the pastor's support. It just never works. A church body can just go as fast and as far in worship as the pastor takes them or encourages you to take them.

Find out how you can support your pastor, share his vision, help his pulpit ministry, amplify his message. Try to get together every week to talk things through and pray together. A congregation always seems to know when you and the pastor are on the same team.

Let's summarize what I've been saying. It comes in three S's:

1. The Spirit of God is ultimately the lead worshiper. By His presence and power, He brings human hearts to God.
2. The worship Servant—which is you, the worship leader—ministers under the authority of the lead pastor to bring worshipers and God together.
3. Now for my last S. (You didn't think I could alliterate like a real preacher, did you?) I'll let this stand for the worship Service itself.

We're finally ready for what you do up on that stage.

Helps for the Worship Service

I've often heard worship leaders say that you really don't need to worry about planning it all out. You just walk up there and go with the Spirit. Well, occasionally this could be the right thing to do. Sometimes it's all you can do. But I've learned that *those who are most prepared are the most led by the Spirit of God*. My caution to you, then, is to be careful not to use the Holy Spirit as an excuse for your laziness. The truth is, the more competent and prepared you are, the more you are able to become invisible. It becomes just the music, the worshiper, and God. That's the real goal of excellence for any worship musician.

So I say, work at it. Practice your craft. Hone your skills. Push yourself. Refine how you work together with your media team, your technicians, and all your support people (they're all part of creating an inviting atmosphere too).

Remember who it is we stand before with our instruments. "Do you see a man skilled in his work?" we read in Proverbs. "He will serve before kings..." (22:29). So if you're wondering how important excellence is for a worship leader, remember the King you serve!

Having said that, I want to close out this chapter focusing on selecting songs and ordering a service.

I'm often asked, "How do you create your set list?" It's a good question. Every leader seems to take a different approach to ordering their songs, and I sure don't think there's one right way. But—be honest now—consider how we create our list most of the time: "Okay, here's five songs we didn't do last week. And here one that's a big hit right now. And here's one that people keep bugging me to play…" And *that* can't be the right way!

Think with me through a few suggestions. I hope you'll find them helpful:

1. Don't start with "We always…" Nothing wrong with traditions—they add richness and continuity and make us feel right at home. But it's a new day. God is doing something, saying something important today that He didn't yesterday. What is it? How can you and your people be part of it? What would happen if…?

That leads us to…

2. Listen for God's heart. This is so important, isn't it? And the only way to have a grasp of what God wants for your people is through time in the Word and in prayer. I admit to being inconsistent with this. But stilling our hearts and minds enough so that we can hear God is a key to effective Christian leadership. Maybe write out your plans, and ask God what He thinks. Then get quiet, wait, and listen.

3. Favor God-focused songs. If you think about it, each song is focused one way or the other—on a human need or feeling or on God. So ask, Is this song God-focused or man-focused?

Overall, I'd say give folks a good balance of both. But if you err, I would err on the side of God-focused songs. That's because the bigger, clearer view we have of God, the more health and truth we'll have in every other situation and relationship. In fact, some of those desperate human "needs" will just melt away.

Go through your library of songs and label each one—God-focused or man-focused. For example, here are a few from my list:

- "Shout to the Lord" (God-focused)
- "I Could Sing of Your Love Forever" (man-focused)
- "Famous One" (God-focused)
- "Open the Eyes of My Heart" (man-focused, God-focused)

4. Keep the motion in mind. After all, you want your songs to take the congregation somewhere, through a series of experiences, and help them arrive at a planned destination.

So ask what each song is accomplishing. What is it creating in the service? Think of your songs as tools. How they are helping you build up the people? For example, is a particular song a song of confession for the audience? Is it a song of preparing our hearts to meet with the Almighty? Once you know what you're building with each song, you should be able to look at your set list and know how the song service will move the people and where they'll arrive at the end.

5. Feel the tempo. Managing the rhythm and tempo of music is so important when you're putting together a dynamic set. One tempo can cause celebration, another contemplation. All of one kind will disappoint your people and end up being counterproductive. For example, you probably don't want to put three or four big anthems together. Or five songs back-to-back at 140 beats per minute (unless someone in the room knows CPR).

6. Think about flow. *Flow*...I love that word. Flo is the name of a girl to me. Sometimes Louie and I do this little thing in a service—we look and listen for Flo.

"Hey, you seen her?" one of us whispers.

"I'm lookin'," whispers the other.

About halfway through the service, we might say, "Oh yeah, she's here all right!" Or maybe it's, "No, don't think Flo's comin' today. Maybe she couldn't find a parking spot." We have so much fun with that.

To me, flow is that sense of grace and purpose that

everyone feels as a strong worship experience unfolds. You're at one as a people, in the moment, in the Spirit...and nothing is hindering you from responding to God.

Flow in a service can be created in so many ways—the key you're playing in, the theme of the songs, how you transition between songs. Take pacing as an example. I think it's important to let songs breathe. What I mean is, not run through them too fast. If it comes to it, it would be more important to let people pause and reflect on a great truth they just sang than for you to get through your whole set.

Flow can be destroyed during the service—at least momentarily—in so many ways. You know the scene:

- A heartfelt song has just ended; people are in deep, quiet reflection...and Eddie Van Lightfingers decides to tune his ax without a mute switch. Real bad for Flo. Better to risk playing the next song out of tune (and next time get a mute pedal).
- Or, song after song, your band is fumbling through the music pages for the next song. Folders drop to the floor, paper flying everywhere. Bad for Flo (I can see her slipping out the back now!). Next time figure out in

advance how your band can move smoothly, invisibly from song to song.

Flow isn't the end-all, of course. Your service can be a disaster and God can still work. But we live in a very distracting world. People arrive at a service needing help to get in a frame of mind that prepares them to meet God. Let's try to create the atmosphere where that is most likely to happen.

7. Teach new songs. New songs breathe life into your ministry. This is an area where you need to lead since you'll get a ton of requests for favorites and few if any for new songs.

But you don't want to create a service where people feel like they're learning—and maybe not succeeding— the entire time. To compensate for this feeling of effort spent, I like to create a moment where people are "free of words." You know, they're not focused on a screen or page, but are able to just let their souls sing out to God. An example would be to follow (or precede) something new with something familiar, like "O Come, Let Us Adore Him." A song like that brings everyone in the room to common ground. Then as people feel comfortable and expressive, you can throw in a new one. It makes the service feel less like a recital.

8. Keep a list of options. With every set list I put together, I always make a separate list of options. Why? 'Cause you want to be ready to adjust if the need arises, or as God moves. More times than not, I find I do go to these options. And remember, if you're using some sort of media presentation, don't leave the media guy in the dark when you get off your set list.

That said, even the option list goes out the window sometimes. I remember one night I had given the band and our media operator the set list for the night, along with another set of songs as options. But by the time I struck the first chord I sensed we should go in a different direction. I didn't play a single song on the list, and I don't think I played anything in a familiar key. The band was playing "Guess the song and guess the key" all night.

Afterward, Jesse walked up and said, "Hey, I'm sure you felt led to go that direction with songs we barely knew and none of them in the right key. Well, we feel led as a band to have you take us to the most expensive steak house in town and buy us all dinner tonight."

That Spirit-led night cost me some cash.

9. "Live it through" before you sing it through. This is all about mental and spiritual preparedness. If I take the time to think about and visualize everything I want to happen *before* it happens, I can be a stronger leader (and, in my case, less nervous). I think of it as doing my part so God can do His part.

Here are some of the things I do before a worship event:

- Think all day about the audience—what their particular needs and expectations might be.
- Spend time with your set list, praying through each song and savoring what it will sound like.

Once I'm at the venue:

- Walk, pray, sing—this does a lot for me.
- Shake my hands to get tension out (it's a nervous habit that the band loves to make fun of me for).
- Study the audience from backstage.
- Visualize what will happen.
- Put everything else out of my mind and walk onstage expecting God to work just like He's promised.

10. Read the audience during the service. Every service has moments…and I watch for them. It's like reading the flow of a river. As you move through the service, things happen, moods change, spiritual desires are awakened. I think God often gifts worship leaders to connect with an audience in such a way that you can sense these moments, then improvise accordingly.

Sometimes I find myself backing away from the lights so I can see. What is happening? (I scan the audience like the beam on a lighthouse sweeping back and forth across the seas.) Are they understanding, responding, leaning forward to what's next? You have to minister to the whole group, not just one or two or the core.

If the audience isn't with me, I "go back and get them." To do that, I might use a verse, a story, a recent insight or teaching I've received. I might just let things breathe and wait for God to move.

Reading the audience is important for worship leaders because music for us isn't the "way I express myself." It's the way we help others express *their* hearts and reach out for God.

COMPETENCE IS NOT A FRUIT

Well, I've talked a lot about the behind-the-scenes work, practice, and planning that goes into a sound worship service. But I want to leave you with a reminder—one that musicians can easily forget. We're so performance oriented. We're so taken up with and moved by beautifully rendered music.

But good worship from an audience is not the same thing as good music. It's not a performance. Ultimately, no one in the room needs a particular talent to impress God or draw close to Him.

One night before a concert, I got an interesting call from my friend Neil. In typical Neil fashion, he shot right past the pleasantries.

"Chris," he said in his raspy voice, "what would it look like if competence was not a fruit of the Spirit?"

That caught me off guard. I mentally reshuffled that well-known list of gifts in Galatians. Nope, no competence there.

"Neil, my friend," I said a little too proudly, "competence *isn't* a fruit of the Spirit."

Neil didn't even hesitate. "But we sure act and teach people like it is," he replied.

I've never forgotten that. I've always felt the pressure to have the right answer, to never be tired, to always be on—platform ready. Can you relate? And yes, I desperately need the fruits of the Holy Spirit—"love, joy, peace, patience, kindness, goodness, faithfulness, gentleness and self control" (Galatians 5:22–23). But I think I'm one of those guys who, somewhere along the way, added "competence" to the

list. And I think a lot of people in the audience can feel hindered for the same reason. They just don't feel good enough to worship God well.

My friend ended the call by saying, "Chris, every once in a while remind the worshipers of God that competence is not a fruit of the Spirit—and watch freedom walk in the room."

The more I've lived with it, the more I believe Neil was right. You don't have to have it all together to be a worshiper of God. None of us do. Not one. By *grace* we all approach the throne of God. We live and breathe in the righteousness and mercy of Jesus.

Just to be part of that amazing event among a great company of others who seek God is what makes worship leaders love what they do...and want to reach for the biggest amps they can get their hands on.

top: Striking the "cool pose" with James Lankford
above: Playing with the Travellers at Rock the Desert, Midland, Texas

CHAPTER SEVEN

THE SONG IN YOU

I'm thinking this chapter should happen around a campfire in the Rockies. Or maybe over some chips and *queso* at Maudie's, a Mexican place I know across the river from here. Or you pick the place.

It should be late at night, a few bugs flying around, a few stars out, no rush—and a bunch of us should be talking, listening, thinking about the road ahead.

Because it's time to talk about the song in you.

Do you know what it is?

I'm crazy enough to believe that there *is* a unique way that each of us finds fulfillment and brings God glory in this life. Getting clarity can be a process, and it usually takes time. As a conversation, it works best in the company of friends. (Chips and *queso* help too.)

By "song in you," I mean a passion or unique ability that seems to have God's signature on it in your life. Mine has been songwriting and leading worship. Your song may be something quite different. Or you may not have a clue *what* it is. Maybe you are sensing God moving you in a certain direction in your life, but you have no idea how to make that happen.

If you feel tangled up in a lot of questions right now, you're not alone. Pretty much by definition, we have more questions than answers in our early years (and later ones too, I'm told). But the questions invite us to lean hard on God. And that's good. God *wants* us to feel our need for Him. That way we give Him room in our lives to show His strength, His provision, His wisdom, His love.

And the questions and unknowns don't have to keep us from going forward with hope. Why? Because the way we were made is a God thing—it's His imprint on our life. He made you and me that way for a purpose. And, "The one who calls you is faithful and he will do it" (1 Thessalonians 5:24).

QUESTIONS, FRIENDS, CHIPS, QUESO

When my friends and I are hanging out late at Maudie's, here are some of the issues we're constantly trying to get our minds and lives around:

"What I'm passionate about doing for God with my life seems so different from what most people do.

Should I pursue it anyway, or stick to something more 'normal'?"

This has been a tough one for me. I didn't come from a family of "professional Christians." My parents loved the Lord, but they had plenty of horse sense too. They couldn't see any more than I could where my music interests might be leading (I mean any direction that might have financial security attached). Besides, I couldn't point to another person I knew who was doing exactly what I wanted to do. And I didn't really have a name—a job title—for it. I didn't want to be a "music minister"—that description just didn't fit me or my personality.

In a situation like that, you can only move forward by faith. And you know, living by faith might sound fun and glamorous. But it isn't. It costs.

Still, I encourage you to be open to your passion and to pursue it as you're able, even if you don't know exactly where it might lead. There is no ranking of passions or gifts in God's family. So whatever it is you want to do with your life, you're not second-rate, and you're not a mistake. And "normal," whatever that is, isn't something God seems to delight in anyway.

If you're wondering why you seem different from those around you, read 1 Corinthians 12 again. Here's just a part of what Paul had to say:

There are different kinds of gifts, but the same Spirit. There are different kinds of service, but the same Lord. There are different kinds of working, but the same God works all of them in all men. (vv. 4–6)

When friends from school were turning into accountants and teachers and investment brokers, I held on to truths like that.

What's the deal with delight?

Another passage I held on to was Psalm 37:4:

Delight yourself in the LORD
and he will give you the desires of your heart.

Even as an eighth grader, that verse became meaningful to me. All through my formative years, I claimed God's promise that He would give me the desires of my heart. Of course, I used to get worried that God might forget. So I'd make a point of reminding Him. "You know my desires, right? You *know* I want to play music. I *love* playing...!" Then I'd quote Psalm 37:4 to God—and wait for the desires of my heart to show up.

Of course, God already knew what I was passionate about—He created me that way, after all. And I was starting at the wrong end of the verse. The bigger truth of the verse is that I must *first* delight in the Lord—trust in Him, give my whole life to Him, treasure what He treasures. Eventually I began to see that when delighting in God becomes my continuing life's objective and passion, God is able to pour out His favor on me in the way He truly desires. And He *does* want to.

"I want to respect the advice of my parents and elders. But I get conflicting opinions. How am I supposed to sort it out?"

No doubt about it, the Bible is packed with reminders to listen to the advice of parents and elders. Here are three verses from Proverbs:

- "A wise son heeds his father's instruction, but a mocker does not listen to rebuke." (13:1)
- "The teaching of the wise is a fountain of life, turning a man from the snares of death." (13:14)
- "Plans fail for lack of counsel, but with many advisers they succeed." (15:22)

God puts us in families for a reason. Sure, there is the odd case of parents or other family members who are permanently clueless. But the exceptions don't disprove the rule: We need our parents, and the younger we are the more closely we should listen to their counsel. It's like learning to ride a bike when you're four or five. You need training wheels to begin with—and you probably need them a little longer than you think you do!

On the conflicting opinions thing—I hate that. I wish there were a single set of GPS life coordinates for your life that you could download and be done with it for the rest of your days. But good can come from wrestling with many viewpoints. It forces us to think and grow, to evaluate our plans and assumptions more carefully. After all, different people have different roles in our lives. They *should* be giving us different perspectives. And besides, no one can be right all the time. Probably that's why the Bible says that "with *many* advisers" you succeed.

Late one night with Dad

I say listen especially carefully to the advice that seems hardest to take. Which brings to mind my father.

As I've already said, Dad is a practical man. For me, that's good, because I tend to go off like a rocket with every new, exciting idea. Early on, when I was pretty sure fame would come knocking any day, Dad kept telling me, "Remember, this is a hobby, son!" He wanted me to head toward a normal, responsible career. But when I was ready to start college, he really supported what God was accomplishing in me. In fact, Dad was the one who gave me a loan to make my first tape. But he'd still say, "Whatever you do, son, just finish your degree."

That was smart advice: Follow your passion *and* keep your head on straight.

But my parents were on a journey of faith too. They were learning right along with me, and their counsel changed as we journeyed together. I remember the night when Dad's wisdom blessed me in an entirely unexpected way.

I was a freshman in college, starting to travel more, getting more invitations, and selling more tapes. I was beginning to think, *I could really do this!* And I really wanted to.

Late one night when I was hanging out down at the pharmacy with my dad, he turned to me and said, "I want you to know that you have my blessing in what you're doing. I can see that this is what you were born to do. It's important for you as my son to know that I love you and support you."

I'll never forget that. His commitment to my music passion—even though it may not have been his first choice for me—made a huge mark on me. I felt like I could do anything.

We stood there and hugged for a long time. Then he said, "But Chris?"

"Yeah, Dad."

"There's one thing…"

"Yeah, Dad."

"Finish that degree!"

"When I think of what I want to pursue, I'm so aware of my limitations. I just feel so ordinary. Why would God have something good ahead for me?" It's easy to look at your abilities and talents compared to others and just shrink in your chair. Plus, I think it's just a natural part of being in the student years that we see everything we *can't* do more clearly than what we *can* do. It can be pretty tough on your morale.

But let's start on the ground. You're not Julia Roberts, Yo-Yo Ma, or Einstein. (How's that for a dose of reality?)

You're also not your brother or your mother. You're not me…

Do you see where I'm going with this? Thanks be to God, you're *you!* The idea of you originated in God's amazingly creative mind. He made you for His own pleasure. Paul wrote, "For from him and through him and to him are all things. To him be the glory forever! Amen" (Romans 11:36).

Could you be a mistake? Not a chance! Makers don't make things for no purpose. And the way you and I were made is valuable. In fact, every one of God's created beings is valuable to Him.

I'll admit, if you believe people are merely an accident of biology or that there's no loving God, none of this will make sense. My prayer is that you will take a few important steps: Ask God to plant a seed of faith in you. Dive into His Word. Be open to His Spirit. And ask Him to make Himself real to you. I promise you that He will.

I've found that when I start envying some other person's gifts, it helps to remember that we all come as package deals. We all have our unusual talents. But we all have our embarrassing, sometimes painful, limitations too. And it's *all* God's plan.

Roger sings it loudest.

I wish you could meet Roger. He's a guy who goes to our church. If you visited, right away you'd hear him singing from wherever you were in the auditorium. Roger sings *loud*. Let me explain.

Roger is bright, funny, and loves God. Roger also suffers from severe cerebral palsy, so he's trapped in a body that doesn't really work. It takes him a while just to get out a few words (which doesn't keep him from trying).

During worship he can't sing at the same pace as everyone else. And what he sings doesn't sound like everyone else either.

Not to worry, Roger sings as best he can (and did I say *loud?*). You should hear it—the sound of Roger praising God. Every Sunday, Roger teaches the rest of us at Austin Stone Community Church what it means to worship.

You and I can't comprehend Roger's day-to-day struggles. He can't take care of himself. He can't even push his own wheelchair. For every necessity—eating, bathing, dressing, getting in and out of bed—he depends on caregivers.

Not long ago, some the guys got together with Roger to produce his testimony on video. They went to his house, recorded him, then headed for the editing studio, and— Roger loves this part of the story—through the magic of technology, Roger's testimony came out pretty smooth.

Here's the last line from what he told us: "I don't know why God made me this way. I'll never know why. But I know that He is good."

Talk about a powerful moment! You and I could sing and talk about the goodness of God all day and never come close. But when Roger declares it out of his utter weakness, people are rocked to the core. Our church needs Roger. He shines the truth where the rest of us can't.

The way you were made—the easy parts, the hard

parts—all fits in God's plan somehow (we'll never know the full story until we get to heaven). Sometimes God will use your strengths. Often He will use your weaknesses. But either way, there are things you can say and people you can say them to that no one else can.

Remember what Peter said to the lame beggar on the temple steps? "Silver or gold I do not have, but what I have I give you. In the name of Jesus Christ of Nazareth, walk" (Acts 3:6).

And you remember what happened next. The man *did* walk. He needed the one thing Peter could do for him more than any riches. And whatever you have to give is God's very best gift for others—probably *many* others—in this world.

So just give it, and watch God go to work.

"I get anxious about my future—not knowing what (if anything) is happening, not feeling like I'm in control of the timing of things. I guess it's a trust issue. Any ideas?"

I can sure relate to this one. I'm an expert at worrying about what's around the next corner. I have to keep coming back to this harsh fact: *Chris Tomlin is not God.* I'm not in charge. I was not made to know my future or to control it. I just need to let go of that deception—confess it as sin.

That's the first step to peace for people like me. Otherwise we'll worry and strive and only end up tired and frustrated.

Even on the days we can't see it, God *is* at work in our lives. Jesus said, "My Father is always at his work to this very day" (John 5:17). Of course, we can't figure out God's ways. He won't be boxed in. He's bigger than all our questions and bigger than our answers.

One thing that's helpful when you can't see what's up ahead is to look back. Most of us can look back and trace the hand of God in our steps. I look back and see that where I am today has not depended on my ability to plan or organize my career. It has been the Lord leading me all the way. He has directed each step.

The fact is, God is always right on time. We can count on it. He knows our heart's deepest desires. He is not some killjoy just playing with our emotions. He holds all of time in His hand. He sees what you and I could never see.

OLD MEN EATING PANCAKES

When things for me are getting vaguer and vaguer, I call to mind a handful of old men in suspenders and work boots eating pancakes…

It's early morning in Sims, Texas, and I've been asked to come and play at a church men's breakfast. I'm about seventeen, it's one of my first gigs, and I've driven three hours to get here.

The thing is, the men aren't that happy to see me—as far as I can tell. They don't know any of the songs I'm playing. They don't sing along. They don't really look at me. They're just busy working their way through plates full of pancakes and eggs and bacon. And I'm sweating my way through my "repertoire" in the corner.

In between songs, there's the sound of chewing…

That's it. That's the whole story. Start to finish—old men chewing food and a disappointed young guitar player wondering why he drove all the way there. What a letdown! What a waste!

But then again, it's not the *whole* story. A man who was there that morning invited me to play somewhere else. And that somewhere else was where I met James Lankford—the crusade preacher you met in chapter 2. And that's when my future as a musician and worship leader started to open up.

Here's the thing: You and I are going to go through any number of days and seasons in our lives when we'll just have no idea what's up. Nothing seems to be happening. Nothing seems to be working.

But God is *always* at work. God will move mountains to put you where He wants you. If God has something that

He wants you to do, He'll give you a platform to do it. One day you'll look back, like I've done lately, and see God's goodness and favor in your life and cry out, "O God, You are amazing! And I love You!"

Paul wrote, "Being confident of this, that he who began a good work in you will carry it on to completion until the day of Christ Jesus" (Philippians 1:6). That's the kind of God we wait on and put our hopes in. He will finish what He's started in our lives.

Our job is to be faithful, to trust Him, to be obedient, to go on. That way we give Him time to do what only He can do—and He does most of His work out of sight and in the strangest ways and places. I say do whatever it takes to remember that. For me, the sound of old men eating breakfast helps.

What sound or story in your life could encourage you to trust God with your future?

Sometimes the reason we don't trust God with our future is that we're not really sure He's as good as we're hoping He is. We think He might be keeping a tally of all our dumb failures and sins. Or that He might have used up all His goodness already on nicer folks.

Ever think that? Then pull on your red sleepers (you know, those pajamas you used to wear with the feet sewn in). It's time for a Tomlin family Christmas story.

THE BIG RIP-OFF

Every Christmas when I was growing up, we'd go for an evening drive to a town near Grand Saline to look at the lights. One house in particular had a reputation for doing up Christmas in a big way. It looked like the Griswold's house in the movie *Christmas Vacation*—everything these folks owned was out in the yard and lit up for maximum effect. The whole sky overhead was ablaze with color. And every year the decorations got bigger and brighter and gaudier.

Driving by the Christmas house had become quite a tradition. Cars would line up for blocks just for a chance to cruise by, gawk, and get that warm holiday feeling.

One year, as our family Chevrolet inched toward the house, we noticed the proud owner of all those lights standing in the yard in front of his house holding out a bucket to each car as it drove past. Mom was driving. Dad was in the passenger seat. And all of us boys were in the back.

Picture what happened next:

"Donna, can you believe this?" Dad exclaimed to my mom. He couldn't believe what he was seeing up ahead. "They've suckered us into coming here all these years, and now that they have this big line of cars, they're asking for *donations*! They're going to make a lot of money off of Christmas!" He was furious.

My brothers and I sat right up. By now we could smell some real Christmas action about to unfold. Mom kept inching the car forward. And Dad just got madder and madder.

The cars were now lined up so tightly that we couldn't turn around. "He's got us!" Dad shouted in utter disbelief and contempt. "We can't even get out of this line! This guy knows exactly what he's doing! He's making all this *money*, for Pete's sake! On families and kids just out to see the lights! Donna…I can't reach my wallet."

Dad's voice trailed off. The sneaky capitalist up ahead was about to rip us off, along with hundreds of other innocent Texas families.

The Chevy inched forward, Dad fumed, and the rest of us barely dared to breathe.

Suddenly, Dad hit on a plan.

"Tell you what I am going to do," he said. "I'm going to roll my window down, and when he sticks his arm in here for the money, I'm rolling it up and he'll get his arm jammed in the window. I'll show him!"

In the backseat, my brothers and I looked at each other, wide eyed. We were all thinking, *This guy's going to lose an arm, and we're all going to jail!*

Sure enough, as we drove up to the house, Dad rolled the window down and slouched in his seat, staring at the floor, ready to strike. When the guy walked toward us, we braced for the worst.

Then we noticed that the bucket was full of candy canes. The man leaned into our window, and with a big smile on his face said, "Y'all have a Merry Christmas. I'm just handing out candy canes to everybody who comes by." And he started handing out candy canes, beginning with the bug-eyed boys in the backseat.

Dad, of course, couldn't bear to accept one.

"Thanks for coming by," the man said cheerily. "Hope you enjoyed the lights. Happy holidays!" Then he walked back toward the next car in line.

We drove by the Christmas house that year in the most *complete* silence.

About a block past the house, Dad finally summoned enough strength to roll his window back up. Pretty soon, the sound of giggling floated up from the backseat. Then we started to laugh.

We laughed all the way home—and it was a one-hour drive—reliving every minute of terror and surprise over and over again. And all the way home, Dad never said a word. He knew he'd been had.

Every Christmas since, one of us boys pops out with a great idea. "Hey Dad," we say, casual as can be, "let's go look at the lights."

But What If...?

Think about it. Most of us go through life convinced that somebody is about to rip us off. We're sure that if we don't watch at every turn, we're going to come out with empty pockets, looking like losers, feeling foolish. And we don't want that to happen!

But what if we bring that same distrustful assumption to what we expect from God for our future?

Seems like it happens a lot. We doubt His goodness. And when we do see His good gifts in our lives, we don't expect them to last. We secretly suspect that He's really just setting us up so He can trap us or pull the rug out from under us. We eyeball every little change or unknown in our lives as new evidence that we're about to get ripped off. We're half waiting for the big laugh from heaven and a voice saying, "Okay, kiddo, the good times are over. Pay up!"

Where is all the suspicion and fear coming from? Sin. Sin has perverted our world and our hearts, and we've become creatures who don't trust our own Creator!

But we'll never realize our God-given destiny unless we live by the truth. And the truth is life changing. Our God is good, and what He does is good (Psalm 119:68). His faithfulness toward each of us is perfect and everlasting (Isaiah 25:1; Psalm 119:90). His kind thoughts toward us are as numberless as all the grains of sand on all the beaches of the world (Psalm 139:17–18). His saving presence is everywhere (Psalm 5:12; 139:7–12).

This God will prove Himself stronger and more generous over the whole course of our lives than we could ever imagine. And you can build a very promising future on that.

THE WORK OF HIS HANDS

We've been thinking through some questions that come up when people wonder how to understand their personal gifts and passions, what to do with them, and how much God might care about it all. I hope you've been encouraged.

Here's one last suggestion. Whenever you wonder what God might have for your future, read all of Psalm 139. David spent a lot of time wondering how such a big, powerful, and loving God could care so much about one puny life. Read Psalm 8, a shorter meditation on the same subject. And you'll be ready to pray this confident prayer of David's from Psalm 138:

> The LORD will fulfill his purpose for me;
>   your love, O LORD, endures forever—
> do not abandon the works of your hands. (v. 8)

Our God is good, and He's at work. Even when we don't know exactly what's ahead, we can still move forward in faith. Enough faith, even, to keep our windows rolled down. Wouldn't want to miss out on any candy canes...

. . . GOD WILL PROVE HIMSELF STRONGER AND MORE
GENEROUS OVER THE WHOLE COURSE OF OUR LIVES
THAN WE COULD EVER IMAGINE. AND YOU CAN
BUILD A VERY PROMISING FUTURE ON THAT.

CHAPTER EIGHT

ROAD MUSIC FOR THIS LIFE

One thing is clear. Life is a never-ending road. Mile after mile of tests, of choosing, of picking up and moving out where the Spirit of God leads you. I don't think true God-followers ever really settle down. Sure, you might live in the same town all your life, but you still never settle down. How can you when you're listening for the wind of God?

This holy wind is always blowing, always putting us in motion in the direction of God's purposes for us. And our purest response is to say "Yes," run our sails up, and go where He takes us. In so many ways, that response is the essence of worship.

I know firsthand what this unsettled life is like. It's risky. It's up and down and most of the time in between. Sometimes you disappoint others and yourself. Sometimes you flat-out fail. But when the critics come around with their pad and pencil to question you about why you did this or that, it's refreshing to just respond, "Look, I took a risk for God, not for myself."

You need faith to live like that, but there's freedom in it too. And you get a front-row seat watching the God of the universe unfolding His plan in your life.

It's the most amazing thing…

"See That Road?"

Can you look back along the road of faith and see how God has graciously led you along? I can.

When I made the choice not to go to grad school, but to trust that God was leading me to travel and play music, it was a risk. There were no guarantees. The next ten years were not mapped out on my apartment wall. But I'm so glad I took the step of faith. I've felt the wind of God blowing many times through that choice, sometimes at almost gale force. I've seen lives change, beginning with mine.

When I got a call from a youth pastor asking me to uproot and move to Houston to help start a new service at a Methodist church, logic argued for a "no." I had never even been in a single Methodist service, for crying out loud! But I heard God whispering. So I rented a U-Haul and off I went. It was a risk, but it was a risk for God. And how much He's blessed me through it! That same youth pastor, Bob Swan, gave me a phone number that led to another phone number—of a bass player named Jesse Reeves. That introduction turned out to be the beginning of a fellowship of friends and players that I call my band today. And so many songs took shape during that season of my life—songs like "Forever," "The Wonderful Cross," "Famous One," and "Be Glorified," to name a few.

When our band was invited to be the worship team for an exciting church plant in Austin, I knew it would be a challenge. Coordinating touring schedules with local church responsibilities can get crazy. But staying meaningfully connected to a local church body matters a lot to me. So in January 2003 our band left Houston and along with Matt Carter and others helped to launch Austin Stone Community Church. We meet at a local high school. We see God's hand at every turn, and we're growing fast.

How would my life be different today if I'd stayed in the comfort of familiar surroundings? Well, more predictable maybe. Yep, more "normal." But a lot more boring too.

I'd rather be in motion with God and His people.

What about you? Think about how different your life could be in one year or five or twenty if you listen carefully for the wind of God in your life and respond. If when the Spirit whispers, "See that road? Take it," you say *yes*.

You could be part of starting something really big. Not

that you'd know it when you walked out the door. God rarely works that way.

He sure didn't with Abraham.

When God Says Leave

You remember Abraham. One day, the wind of the Spirit gusted into his life. God said:

> "Leave your country, your relatives, and your father's house, and go to the land that I will show you. I will cause you to become the father of a great nation. I will bless you and make you famous, and I will make you a blessing to others. I will bless those who bless you and curse those who curse you. All the families of the earth will be blessed through you. (Genesis 12:1–3, NLT)

We don't know exactly what Abraham did next. Did he run God's message past his accountant? Did he think about it for days or weeks? Did he finish getting his degree?

Don't know.

But here's what we do know: "So Abram departed," the Bible says, "as the LORD had instructed him" (v. 4).

When God says, "Leave," are you ready to hit the road?

He's probably not going to ask you to walk out of your

dorm room or apartment today. More often He'll ask you to leave behind comfortable assumptions, competing commitments, mixed-up priorities, a wrong relationship, a "must have" list of conditions.

We just can't go down the road with God with all that baggage.

But when we say yes to God's invitations, big things happen—or at least become possible for the first time. Look at what God accomplished through Abraham and his descendants. Through the Jewish people, Jewish law, the Bible, and the Messiah Himself, God has indeed blessed all the people of the earth.

I'll be honest, God has never walked into my room to deliver an exact set of directions for what I should do next and why. Wouldn't it be nice! But if I've discovered that if I listen, God leads me just the same. By the Spirit's presence, by His Word and His people, and in so many other ways…God walks in!

I refer to these calls or revelations from God in my life as awakenings, or grace moments.

FLASHBULB MOMENTS

They are that flashbulb-goes-off kind of experience. What only a minute ago seemed like a blur suddenly snaps into focus. In this book, I've shared several of those grace moments in my life. I'm sure you can point to moments of your own.

Recently I had another one.

I'd been rethinking the whole business side of Christian music—the touring, the promoting, the marketing. Then, in a conversation someone said, "The only reason a musician tours is to sell a new record." Instinctively I agreed and went on about my day. But it didn't take long for that beautiful, disciplining whisper to make itself heard in my soul. I was driving in my car. Like a sheep hears the shepherd, I heard these words: *The reason you tour is not to sell records. The reason you tour is to share Me with everyone you can.*

Wow! That cleared things up!

One of the earliest flashbulb moments I can remember is when I read an unusual verse in Numbers. The verse records God's opinion of one man, Caleb. I've never forgotten what I read:

> Because my servant Caleb has a different spirit and follows me wholeheartedly, I will bring him into the land he went to, and his descendants will inherit it. (14:24)

Just reading those words "Caleb has a different spirit" turned on lights all over the place for me. They stirred a huge desire in my heart to be that man, to have God feel that way about me—not just after I'm dead, but every day of my life now.

Caleb, as you might know, was one of twelve soldiers Moses sent to spy out the Promised Land before Israel invaded it. But of the twelve, only Caleb and Joshua came back with good news. Yes, they'd seen giants, walled cities, and huge armies. But, said the two men, the land itself was just as beautiful as God had said. And God had promised to give it to them.

Their recommendation to Moses and all the people was: "With God, let's go!" (Can't you hear the music from *Braveheart* playing in the background?)

But sadly, Israel listened to the doubters. The nation turned back from its destiny, suffered God's anger, and wasted forty years in the desert.

I'd rather be the guy with "a different spirit."

I'd rather keep my heart and mind fixed on what is unseen. If ten turn back with excuses and distractions, I'd rather be among the two who say, "With God, let's go!"

How about you?

ALL OF ME, ALL MY DAYS, ALL FOR HIM

You've come with me this far in the pages of this book because you care a lot about the promises of God for your life. But now it's time to decide. And I can't put the decision you face any more clearly than Paul did:

> Therefore, I urge you, brothers, in view of God's mercy, to offer your bodies as living sacrifices, holy and pleasing to God—this is your spiritual act of worship. (Romans 12:1)

For several years, this verse has been my standard definition of what it means to live wholeheartedly for God's glory—all of me (my body, mind, and heart), all my days (a living sacrifice), all for Him (holy and pleasing to God).

And what does Paul call that kind of life?

My spiritual act of worship!

A whole generation of Christ's followers is having an awakening moment on this issue. I've met thousands of them. They're waking up to the fact that only a few things in life will last forever—and they want to figure out what they are. They see the hollowness of selfish goals, even of selfish Christianity. They sense that there's more to what God is doing in our time, on our planet—and they want to be part of it.

Matt Redman captures it this way in his song "The Heart of Worship":

When the music fades
All is stripped away
And I simply come
Longing just to bring
Something that's of worth
That will bless Your heart

I'll bring You more than a song
For a song in itself
Is not what You have required
You search much deeper within
Through the way things appear
You're looking into my heart

I'm coming back to the heart of worship
And it's all about You
It's all about You, Jesus
I'm sorry, Lord, for the thing I've made it
When it's all about You,
It's all about You, Jesus

Of course, it's a big decision—*all of me, all my days, all for Him*. But as Louie says, "You *are* a worshiper. Worship is what you do." It's the way we were made.

I know from my own experience that the college years are the best time to get these things settled. Not when you're forty and you've built a whole life on self and now you have to keep it from crashing. Not when you're seventy and most of your opportunities are behind you.

But I've seen so many in my generation getting things settled—responding in hushed awe to the God who made them to worship Him, and who is calling them lovingly to Himself.

With thousands, I've seen it happen by candlelight.

CLOUD OF WITNESSES

It's a service called "the lighting of the lamps," a worship tradition among followers of Christ that dates back to the earliest years of the church. At that time, a candle was always kept burning at the site of Christ's tomb. Believers would light a candle at the tomb, then take it into their church at the start of evening prayers to begin their service. Then they'd sing a hymn, which came to be known as the "*Phos Hilaron*" (Greek for the opening words of the hymn).

The words of this ancient hymn go like this:

Hail, gladdening Light, of His pure glory poured
Who is the immortal Father, heavenly, blest,
Holiest of Holies, Jesus Christ our Lord.

Now we are come to the sun's hour of rest,
The lights of evening round us shine,
We hymn the Father, Son, and Holy Spirit divine...

Don't you feel hushed, bowed, awed by those words? I do. And they've been calling Christ's followers into worship for generations.

That's why on a recent Passion tour we revived the "Phos Hilaron" tradition as a way of beginning each concert. The lights dimmed. The crowd hushed. Then, in the silence, a person walked down the aisle from the back, bringing a lighted lamp to set on the stage.

A simple ceremony. Yet it is a powerful reminder that Jesus, the Light of the World, is risen, and He is among us as we worship.

The original melody of the "Phos Hilaron" hasn't survived the years—all we have is the words. So night after night on tour, we'd light the lamps, then say the words together.

Hail, gladdening Light, of his pure glory poured
Who is the immortal Father, heavenly, blest,
Holiest of Holies, Jesus Christ our Lord.

That little resurrected tradition of the church has led to a new CD project, *Hymns Ancient and Modern: Live*

Songs of Our Faith. Under Louie's guidance, the project brings together lead worshipers Matt Redman, the David Crowder Band, Charlie Hall, Nathan and Christy Nockels, and me.

Here's the thing: Young people these days don't want a faith that's just the latest thing. They're excited to know that we stand in a long line of worshipers—a huge cloud of witnesses—who have gone before. To recite the "Phos Hilaron" together or to sing the doxology is a moving way of saying, "Wow, my faith is not something I made up! It has endured for two thousand years!"

And we want to do our part to recapture its power and passion...and pass it on.

RETURNING THE GIFT

I hope these few pages have given you a new sense that God created you with something *huge* in mind and that He's specially gifted you to respond to Him with all of you, for all of your life...and on into eternity. Don't let that moment of creation with your name on it go to waste for another day.

That our loving God would make us in His image, think of us, and give His life to ransom us back to Himself shows just how much you and I are worth in His eyes. Does

God really need me? I don't think so. But He made us for Himself nevertheless. I can't really explain it. But I know it's true!

He made us.

He saves us.

He calls us.

And He gifts us…to worship Him with our whole being forever.

Only God can satisfy our soul. Fame, wealth, relationships, and success just aren't going to do it for long. You and I were made for something more.

With God, let's go. We don't have to be someone we're not. Or wait until we finally have it all together (and a long, long wait that would be).

We just need to respond to His greatness, giving back to Him in worship His miracle in us, and set out on the road.

THE WAY I WAS MADE

Caught in the half light
I'm caught alone
Waking up to the sunrise
And the radio
Feels like I'm tied up
What's holding me
Praying today will be the day I go free

I want to live like there's no tomorrow
I want to dance like no one's around
I want to sing like nobody's listening
Before I lay my body down
I want to give like I have plenty
I want to love like I'm not afraid
I want to be the man I was meant to be
I want to be the way I was made

Made in Your likeness,
Made with Your hands
Made to discover,
Who You are and who I am
All I've forgotten,
Help me to find
All that You've promised let it be in my life

I want to live like there's no tomorrow
I want to dance like no one's around
I want to sing like nobody's listening
Before I lay my body down
I want to give like I have plenty
I want to love like I'm not afraid
I want to be the man I was meant to be
I want to be the way I was made

CONVERSATIONS

a study guide for personal or group use

PREFACE & CHAPTER 1:
THE SOUND YOU HEAR

Summary: Chris invites the reader to join other followers of Jesus who have chosen worship as a way of life.

Big Idea: You and I have been made by God for a big purpose—"to spread the fame of Jesus everywhere we go." This is worship as a way of life. There's a growing movement of young believers who are getting passionate (and loud!) about lifting up God's name and honor. It's a shared mission, but we each have unique gifts, interests, and opportunities. Why? Because our amazing Creator made us to express our mission in our own, one-of-a-kind way too.

1. Do you feel free to be the way you were made? Talk about your response.

2. Do you believe that your worship—whether you sing it, play it, or live it—has the power to influence others? Why or why not?

3. Have you been part of a worship event where you felt God's presence in a memorable way? If so, try to describe how your experience affected you.

4. Why do you think some people have such a hard time figuring out why a person would get excited about worship?

5. In your own life, what "created things" tend to take the place of the Creator as the focus of your attention? (See Romans 1:21, 25.)

6. Chris writes, "Listen, God didn't make a mistake when He made you. He didn't set out to make another Einstein…only to get interrupted, say, or have a bad day." Are there certain people or situations that tend to make you feel like a mistake or second class? If so, can you identify a reason? What might the God of Psalm 139:13–14 want you to know next time you feel that way?

CHAPTER 2: SALT OF THE EARTH

Summary: Chris takes the reader back to his small hometown of Grand Saline, Texas, to retrace how God led him from his first guitar lesson as a nine-year-old to his ministry of songwriting and leading worship today.

Big Idea: You don't have to be rich, famous, or supertalented for God to come knocking on the door of your life. If you're open to His Spirit, God will bring people into your life—parents, friends, mentors—who will help you make the right decisions and move you in the direction He has for you. Even those big, fat failures or embarrassments don't have to hold you back. Turn your life and your dreams over to God, listen carefully for His leading, and He'll walk with you toward your future.

1. "Like most kids growing up, I didn't know that God was near," Chris writes. Thinking of your own childhood or teen years, would you agree or disagree with Chris? Why?

2. Have you ever had an "I belong to You now" experience with God? If so, what happened? How has that decision affected your life since?

3. Try to identify the people in your past who have helped you get a better grasp on an important

personal interest or ability. What did they do or say that was so effective?

4. Have you been afraid to pursue what you're *really* passionate about? If so, why? Do you think any of your "good" reasons to be afraid might actually be rooted in pride?

5. Most Christians believe that God loves them (after all, He loves the whole world). But do you think God actually *likes* you? Do you think He likes you enough to have a good future in mind for you? Explain your answers. (For some Bible insights on this issue, read Psalm 31:19; 86:5; Jeremiah 29:11; Matthew 7:11; Luke 15:11–32; James 1:5, 17.)

Chapter 3: Made for His Glory

Summary: "Talking about who God is and how I wrote my songs about Him go together," writes Chris. So in this chapter, he takes the reader on what he calls a "songwriting road trip," using stories of some of his best known songs to lead into a discussion of the nature of God.

Big Idea: Before you and I get far in giving away our life for God's glory, we have to answer the question: *So who is this*

God we are supposed to center our lives around? What we discover when we sincerely pursue knowing God is that He is greater and more loving than we could ever imagine or hope. Though He is holy, He still invites us into forgiveness and fellowship. And He is more than enough for our every need.

1. A Texas thunderstorm helped Chris get a bigger view of God's greatness. Can you describe a similar experience that stretched your idea of God?

2. Share a favorite Bible passage that describes God's glory and greatness (some ideas—Genesis 1; Job 38–41; Psalm 104; Isaiah 6; Isaiah 53; Romans 8). Which aspect of God's nature seems most meaningful to you today?

3. How could a deeper understanding of God's holiness make a difference in your life?

4. When we get overwhelmed with daily pressures, we can easily make decisions as if our "now" is more important and real than our eternity. How could you do better at keeping the "forever-ness" of God and your eternal future as His child in mind each day?

5. If a person were to look down on your life over the last week, would he or she decide that you

really do believe that "God is enough"? Explain your answer. Do you think God is asking you to make a change?

CHAPTER 4:
LIFESTYLES OF THE UNNOTICED

Summary: From his perspective of a life in the spotlight, Chris talks about the appeal and the lie of living for fame. He describes how he wrote the song "Famous One," then shares stories of "unnoticed" people who have deeply influenced him.

Big Idea: Fame is a big deal to a lot of people today, but it can do huge damage to your sense of reality. The only way to deal with a desire to be in the spotlight is to keep Jesus there—where He belongs—because He is the only truly famous One. Where does that leave you and me? Living a humble, unnoticed—and very powerful—life for God.

1. If you had to pick one, would you say you are more tempted by fame, money, pleasure, or power? How can each of those idols make us say *adios* to reality and act like a fool?

2. It's politically correct to think of Jesus as a great teacher or enlightened being. But what are some

creative ways you could introduce your non-Christian friends to the Jesus at whose name every knee will one day bow?

3. Humility is one of those qualities that if you think you have it…you probably don't. Where does a lifestyle of humility come from?

4. Neil bought expensive cigarettes for a waitress to make an important point. Do you agree with his strategy? Any ideas on how you could use a more daring approach to share Christ?

5. What grandparent or other older person in your life has had the most impact on your beliefs and lifestyle today? Share your stories.

CHAPTER 5: THE NOISE WE MAKE

Summary: Chris describes a church concert where feelings against amplified worship music ran strong. Then he discusses some Bible teachings on worship styles.

Big Idea: People worship God in different ways, but the Bible *does* have some things to say about what worship expressions we should hold in common. For example:

- "lift your hands"
- "bow down"
- "be still before Him"
- "shout for joy"
- "dance"

However we choose to worship, it's still all about Jesus, and true worship will always draw us closer to Him.

1. Ever run into a person or group who behaved like self-appointed worship police? If so, what happened? What did you learn?

2. Which worship expression is most challenging for you? Which is most natural? Why?

3. Do you feel less "spiritual" because you feel guarded or awkward about certain worship expressions? Or do you feel at peace about it before the Lord?

4. Tell about a time when something so wonderful happened to you that you couldn't keep from shouting or dancing with joy. Ever had a similar experience in your relationship with God?

5. Write your own version of Psalm 117 (at just two verses, it's the shortest psalm in the Bible). In this psalm, the writer cites two reasons for calling people to worship: the Lord's love and the Lord's faithfulness. What are yours?

CHAPTER 6: SPIRIT OVERFLOW

Summary: Here, Chris is talking mainly to those who lead corporate worship. He gives pointers on how a leader can prepare, respond to the Spirit, work well with a pastoral team, and deliver a God-honoring worship experience.

Big Idea: We're all called to lift up the name of Jesus every day, but some of us are also called to lead others in worship in a public setting. Leading worship is an important ministry—for one thing, because people come to a service distracted, resisting, tired, worried, or not even interested. Ultimately, only God's Spirit is able to bring us to God. But a sensitive and prepared worship team can do a lot to invite others into this wonderful encounter.

1. What are some ways we can easily get confused about what is really happening in a high-energy worship concert?

2. How have you sensed the Spirit leading you or speaking to you during worship? How would you advise another person on discerning what is truly Spirit and what is something else?

3. What are some words you would use to describe worship leaders or worship services that have been most helpful for you?

4. What are some of the things you like *least* about worship leaders or services?

5. Talk about Neil's challenge to Chris: "Competence is not a fruit of the Spirit—but we sure act and teach people like it is." How would you apply that advice in your life?

CHAPTER 7: THE SONG IN YOU

Summary: "It's time to talk about the song in you," writes Chris. Then he talks through some common questions that come up when people are coming to grips with what God wants them to do with their interests and abilities.

Big Idea: You don't have to sing well, write songs, or play guitar to honor God with the way you've been made. Each of us has been uniquely gifted to celebrate God's fame in our generation. As we value and pursue our individual path to a life of worship, we can be confident that God is passionately involved in the outcome.

1. If you were to put in a sentence or two the life direction or set of gifts you feel God wants to bless most in your future, what would you say?

2. Do you struggle with feeling different from, or inferior to, others? If so, where do you think those feelings come from? What do you think God wants for you in these areas?

3. What one circumstance or limitation seems like the biggest obstacle between you and the future God wants for you? Describe it for others in your group and ask for their perspectives.

4. Who are the people you most often turn to for godly wisdom? Why? Have you told them recently how important they are to you?

5. When you think about your future, what do you worry about most? Read Matthew 6:19–34 and Philippians 4:4–9. Write out your worry and what these verses tell you about how to deal with it. Then consider signing and dating your statement and prayerfully surrendering your worry to God.

6. Read "The Big Rip-Off" story aloud. Have you ever felt totally distrustful about what God was up to in your life? Describe what happened and what you learned.

CHAPTER 8: ROAD MUSIC FOR THIS LIFE

Summary: Chris leaves the reader with encouragement, a challenge to decide, and a place to start.

Big Idea: Life is a never-ending road, and God's holy wind is always blowing. How should we keep moving toward the future God wants for us? By faith—and that means taking some risks. Fortunately, God promises us His blessing and gives us "awakening moments" when He makes His will plain to us. Along the way, we must offer ourselves in daily sacrifice to Him. Ultimately, that's the only way we can experience the full life Jesus promised.

1. We all respond differently to change and to sameness in our lives. Would you say you have more trouble "leaving" for God or "staying" for God? Talk about your answer.

2. Chris talks about having "flashbulb-goes-off" experiences, where God gave him a key insight or

leading. Have you experienced something similar? If so, describe it and what it means to you now.

3. The example of Caleb—who had "a different spirit and follows me wholeheartedly"—is important to Chris. Is there a Bible character or life verse that you're taking with you on your journey?

4. Look again at Romans 12:1: "Therefore, I urge you, brothers, in view of God's mercy, to offer your bodies as living sacrifices, holy and pleasing to God—this is your spiritual act of worship." Have you personally and decisively given yourself and your future over to God? If not, what is holding you back?

5. If you started today offering yourself to God as a living sacrifice, what do you think God could accomplish in you, and for you, and through you in five years? In forty years? Consider finding other passionate disciples of Jesus who will wholeheartedly commit to traveling that road with you, starting today.

CHRIS TOMLIN DISCOGRAPHY

SOLO PROJECTS

2004 *Arriving*, sixstepsrecords/Sparrow Records
2002 *Not to Us*, sixstepsrecords/Sparrow Records
2001 *The Noise We Make*, sixstepsrecords/Sparrow Records

COMPILATIONS AND OTHER RECORDINGS

2004 *Passion: Hymns Ancient & Modern: Live Songs of Our Faith*, sixstepsrecords/Sparrow Records (CD)
2004 *In the Name of Love: Artists United for Africa*, Sparrow Records (CD)
2004 *Worship Together: Here I Am to Worship*, Worship Together (CD)
2004 *WOW Worship: Red*, Word/Provident/Sparrow Records (CD)
2003 *Passion: Sacred Revolution—Songs From OneDay03*, sixstepsrecords/Sparrow Records (CD/DVD)
2003 *Wait for Me: The Best from Rebecca St. James*, ForeFront Records
2003 *Worship Together: I Could Sing of Your Love Forever*,

Time Life (CD)

2003 *Wow Worship: Yellow*, Word/Provident/Sparrow Records (CD)

2003 *New Song Cafe DVD* (vols. 1–4), Worship Together (DVD)

2002 *Passion: Our Love Is Loud*, sixstepsrecords/Sparrow Records (CD)

2000 *Passion: OneDay Live*, sixstepsrecords/Sparrow Records (CD/DVD)

2000 *Passion: Road to OneDay*, sixstepsrecords/Sparrow Records (CD)

SONGBOOKS

Arriving

Passion: Hymns Ancient & Modern

DigiSongbook: Songs for the Passion Generation

Passion: Sacred Revolution

Worship Together: Here I Am to Worship

Worship Together 5.0

Worship Together: I Could Sing of Your Love Forever

Passion: Our Love Is Loud

The Noise We Make

CCLI Songs and Ranking

"Forever" #10

"We Fall Down" #14

"The Wonderful Cross" #27

"Famous One" #47

"Enough" #58

"Be Glorified" #109

"Holy Is the Lord" #152

"Kindness" #218

"Wonderful Maker" #277

"Not to Us" #296

"Unchanging" #302

"Take My Life" #311

"The Noise We Make" #430

Awards

Worship Leader magazine Praise Awards:

- 2003 Best Scripture Song "Holy Is the Lord," *Passion: Sacred Revolution—Songs from OneDay03*
- 2002 Best New Song "Enough," *Not to Us*

Dove Award Nominations:

- 2004 Special Event Album of the Year, *Passion: Sacred Revolution—Songs From OneDay03*
- 2003 Praise & Worship Album of the Year, *Not to Us*
- 2003 Special Event Album of the Year, *Passion: Our Love Is Loud*

TOURS

2004 Fall 2004/Spring 2005 "All Things New" tour with Steven Curtis Chapman

2003 Passion Experience Tour—80,000-plus attended, garnered *New York Times* story

2003 iWorship Tour

2003 OneDay03 gathering (Sherman, Texas)—20,000-plus college students attended

2002 40-plus tour dates with Rebecca St. James

2000 OneDay gathering (Memphis, Tennessee)—40,000-plus college students attended

Links

www.christomlin.com

Check out my website for news, concert schedule, bios, discography, e-mail, and store.

www.268generation.com

The on-line community for the Passion conferences, Passion Worship CDs, OneDay Gatherings, speaking series and DVD from Louie Giglio and others, an events calendar, and the musicians and ministry associated with the Passion Movement. Don't miss Louie's Journal.

www.sixstepsrecords.com

The label, now sixstepsrecords/Sparrow Records, presents the music of lead worshipers of the Passion Movement, including Chris Tomlin, the David Crowder Band, Charlie Hall, Matt Redman, and worship compilations like *OneDay Live* and *Hymns Ancient and Modern*.

www.theaustinstone.com

See what God is doing in the city of Austin at the Austin Stone Community Church, a growing young church plant. Stephen F. Austin High School, 6 P.M. Sundays, is the place. And I'm usually leading worship.

Acknowledgments

T hank you, David Kopp, for making sense out of my ideas and being a great friend in the writing and editing process.

Thank you, Shelley, for continuing to sharpen me and for helping me write this book.

Thank you, Louie, for encouraging me to go beyond just a guitar and a song, but to pass on what God has taught me so far.

Thank you to all those who have walked parts of this road with me—Jesse and Janet Reeves, Daniel Carson, J. D. and Tiffani Walt, James Lankford, my EMI and sixsteps family, Bob Swan, Matt Carter, David Crain, Joey Humke, Matt Redman… It's an honor.